Finding My Way

Joe Wise

BALBOA.PRESS

A DIVISION OF HAY HOUSE

Scripture quotations are from the ESV® Bible (The Holy Bible, English Standard Version®), copyright © 2001 by Crossway, a publishing ministry of Good News Publishers. Used by permission. All rights reserved.

Balboa Press books may be ordered through booksellers or by contacting:

Balboa Press
A Division of Hay House
1663 Liberty Drive
Bloomington, IN 47403
www.balboapress.com
844-682-1282

Print information available on the last page.

ISBN: 978-1-9822-6755-1 (sc)
ISBN: 978-1-9822-6756-8 (e)

Balboa Press rev. date: 04/27/2021

I wish I could show you
when you are lonely
or in darkness
the astonishing light of your own being.
Hafiz

To Alicia,
      bold bearer of Truth and Beauty.
And to John Pell,
      the symphony of him.

Contents

About the Cover

It was hot, the first time I entered Antelope Canyon. "It" is the July Arizona sun. "It" is the burning sand under my Asics. "It" is my body. "She"—and this is a distinctly feminine experience for me—*she* was cool. Cave cool. Soothing cool. Wait. Can a canyon be a cave? I am standing in one. Drawing cooler air into my lungs. Removing my wrap-around sunglasses. Feeling my unconscious heat-tenseness release. Refuge. And soon—beauty. Beyond description. I live amid the red rock splendor of Sedona. A wide open gallery of jewels. Lit by this planet's biggest, brightest unfiltered light. Here, in this slot in the earth, this light has only a crack to illuminate through. But the dance it does in interplay with rock is cave-bustingly beautiful.

In beauty we walk. Unlike The Grand, there is no wide shot whole-istic wow for eyes and soul. It is a walk. A path. Turns. And twists. Each step inviting a pause, a stay. Unlike Mammoth or Carlsbad, it is intimate. You can and do touch either wall of this rarified ribbon, and know its surprising softness. Rock, appearing as soft, spun, velvety fabric. Spun and loomed by its years of channeling life-giving water, in a high hot desert.

I have gone to "her" in different seasons and contrasting days. Her raiment's tone and colors vary. There remains one particular spot where at high noon or thereabouts, the master light shines directly down into her. The rest is diffused, often subtle, splashes of 10,000 hues. In semi darkness. This is why I chose this capture, this photo, by a world class photographer and a deep heart friend, Larry Lindahl.[1]

It speaks to my continual journeys of walking out of the dark towards the light, even as the dark blesses me with its wonders.

> *In beauty I walk.*
> *As I walk, as I walk,*
> *The universe is walking with me.*
> *In beauty it walks before me.*
> *In beauty it walks behind me.*
> *In beauty it walks below me.*
> *In beauty it walks above me.*
> *In beauty I walk.*[2]

In beauty *we* walk. Finding our way.

★　★　★

And the **back cover** photo, of me presenting at a Pumphouse event, was taken by Gary Every,[3] prolific writer, raconteur extraordinaire, and the pilot and heart of Sedona's Poetry and Prose Project, which he uses to keep the written word in any form, out loud, that is, performed, as well as a venue to foster emerging writers as they seek to find *their* way.

Preface

Everyday Spirituality was my working title for this collection. It never left. It has a certain redundancy to it, a mental "du-uh." What other kind is there? Is there ever a time we're not human? Is there ever a time we're not divine? Who gets to say what's mundane? What's sacred?

We all do. Minute by minute. Day by day. I still have a subconscious playbook that surfaces with things like, "I'm waiting for something holier." Or "I'll be fine when I'm more...better...or different." Or "as soon as Covid is over."

What I'm discovering is, I don't know much about any of this, and I'm most at peace when I let everything be, just as it is. Let the delights be delights. Let the thorns be thorns. And if I live in my heart, I'm home. If I *lead* with my heart in response to the world around me, I stay centered, in tune, and find somehow I am a beneficial presence. As Mooji teaches, "If Consciousness had no use for it, it wouldn't happen." This includes me. My expression of the divine. God being me on planet earth.

We're all in this together. This is a dimension of awakening to the Truth of Being. A hard one to swallow sometimes, because it slays one of the most precious-to-us parts of our ego. Simultaneously it opens us up to the fullness of creation and lets us embrace and be embraced by the infinite beauty and wonders of the earth and its peoples. An ancient wisdom teaching: God (the only and all Reality) sleeps in stones. Stirs in plants. Dreams in animals. Awakens in humans.

Introduction

Breathe.
Breathe.
Just breathe.
In and out.
Deep and slow.
Breathe.

Reminders from everywhere of the preciousness of breath. From spilling-over I.C.U.s, to one man's knee on another man's neck.

Being careful *where* you breathe. Deep gratitude that you *can* breathe, and finding safe places to do so. Giving others space, while attending to your own.

I don't *"beat"* my heart. I *can* breathe my breath. At least make choices on individual breaths. Depth. Duration. It is *still* in the divine dance. I breathe Life. Life breathes me.

This in the middle of every "Blursday," (as one reporter called it). Cloistered. Not clustered. More and more invitations into the now-ness of my life. The "chop wood and carry water" components of my life. Even as we add in, in our "public" life, two new numbers to our collective traumas, wounds, inflection points, stimulants to change. To go with 9/11 and before. We add 8:46[4] and 1/6. Two "new" experiences to unpack as we dare. A time to die, and a day to insurrect.

All reminding me, I/we are always finding our *way*. In unpredictable *ways*. With halts and starts. Clumsiness and grace. The mystery remains. And so do we.

The phenomenon of a Covid "year," in all its dimensions, prompted me to drop my working title for this book, and place instead *Finding My Way* on its cover as the best way to name my current knowing. And *not* knowing.

As Grace would have it, Sir Paul decided to do a Covid-time solo album. It would include, "Find My Way." Lending his hand to help me reach "the love I feel inside." While I, as an old white dude, with a soul as young as any, stand with Amanda, a young African American woman, with a soul as old as any, as we all wittingly or unwittingly, consciously or unconsciously help each other find our way.

When day comes, we step out of the shade of flame and unafraid.
The new dawn balloons as we free it.
For there is always light, if only we're brave enough to see it.
If only we're brave enough to be it.[5]

–Amanda Gorman
America's first youth poet laureate

How Are You?

"How are you?"

"I'm finding my way," she says as she steps back from our hug and my question. She is about two years away from the loss of her, what…companion? Friend? Split-apart? Buddy? Love?

"All the above." She would say if I asked. "Soul mate" would be too tripe for her, but it would be true. Clifford. A man of humor (extra dry), presence (extra steady), insight, care, and simple kindness. Clifford would have worn the tee shirt I had just seen minutes ago at the gym—"Be present. Not perfect."

I am reminded of my therapist's question when I came to him in my forties with a string of deaths on *my* belt, each trailing its invisible anchor. "Do you know how long most people give another to grieve a major loss?"

"Three months?" I venture, with no calendar awareness connected to any of mine, and trying to be generous.

"That's right," he says. "Actual time runs more like three *years*. All my shame, or almost all, about not being "over it yet" melted down, if not away. Being male and being strong for me meant mostly holding *my* emotions *in* and holding *up* the "weaker (meaning mostly crying) sex" and /or "the young."

There were way too many traps here for me to have any desire, or impulse, much less permission, to *find out* how *I* grieve. As with most significant human experiences, I learn, there are *some* patterns and, especially in this case (letting go of something or someone big) *wide* variants. My first step was to de-equate weakness or lack of strength with crying. Which opened out a whole paradoxical universe exploring vulnerability as strength. And, the biggest surprise of all, a bridge to intimacy. I would learn and reinforce these "truths" with my life companion, and friends. Finding, strangely, the hardest person to "practice" them with was myself. Understandably now, as I see the enculturation more clearly. And the familial patterns. Pursuing stasis in the realm of boundaries *and* vulnerability became high-wire Wallenda-like experiments. Some, *completely* netless.

I am remembering a moment I was glad for my work in these arenas. My friend Charlie had lost a dear friend, a canine companion. I walked up to him and embraced him. He cried in my arms. My own sadness and losses slowly rose up, and I did the unthinkable. I cried *with* him. I didn't feel strong. I didn't feel weak. I felt human. And authentic.

Grieving, as we now know from Elisabeth Kübler-Ross's seminal work, has a more or less evolutionary pattern. Stages even. I know it now from my own experience. Losing someone close to me, best friend close, when I was 26. Eclipsing in strength and depth, the loss of my grandparents in my teens and early 20s. In my grief work, with latent residue, 20 years later, I came to know how much I missed the *mirror* of him, Johnny. How clearly I saw in him all the things in *me* I loved, and had in some ways cloaked over, left un-nurtured, or felt "unworthy" of. Basically, dimming down the incandescence I had known in him and in myself out of what…respect for the dead? "Appropriate" affect? Survivor guilt? Repressed anger over the felt-abandonment? Of course it was all the above and then some.

I had, in a couple of years, lost my best friend, and my (I felt) life's purpose—to be a priest.

I know God is no respecter of person's and His "rain falls on the just and the unjust." But *within the year* I got a lightning bolt that felt like it had only my name on it. Maleita. *And* a path to begin to do the work I felt sent here to do, and *wanted* to do—*with her*. Two crushing losses on a wave coming in, and almost instantly, magically a bright-souled companion and an illumined evolving path on the same wave's return to the whole. The whole of the sea. The whole of life, all of it mixed together in inscrutable and oceanically unfathomable ways.

I *do* know I'm sometimes finding my way and sometimes my way is finding me. I *do* know the first way, the former, is the easiest. It's the one that contributes most generously to my phantom "I'm-in-control" account.

I *do* know when somebody asks me, "How's it goin'?" I can almost always say, It's goin' good. *I'm* just not so good at goin' along."

And thanks to Sherry, the lady in my hug and question ("How are you?"), I've decided that instead of "fine" or "Ok" or even "lousy," I'm setting my new default response at "I'm finding my way."
And thanks to a Clifford-like tee shirt, setting my new default *religion* at "Be present. Not perfect."

I Say

I say what I need to hear.
I teach what I need to learn.
I point to that which I hold as True, no matter the degree of realization.

If on a Winter's Night

by Italo Calvino

This is from writers group. We chose a title from The Guardian's *list of the 100 greatest novels of all time, and wrote for twenty minutes.*

Karl Rahner, the famous German theologian, has set forth his views on spirituality in a dual season metaphor. Summer spirituality and Winter spirituality. Summer is—the sun is out and bright and you are on a beach. And everybody is playing, basking, building sand castles. "God's in His heaven. And all is right with the world."[6]

Winter spirituality is—you are trekking alone, at night, in the woods. It is cold and dark. Once in a while you see a distant cabin, with warm yellowish light emanating from its window panes. You walk over toward it, come up to the sill and peek in. There is a fire in the fireplace. The people are warm and content. You nod your head to yourself and go back to the journey.

Like most attempts to "capture" phenomena, this one limps. But it's fine for reminding us this is more complex and diverse than often taught. *And* comforting to be assured one size does not fit all, we can have a predominance of one season, *and* can know the unnamed seasons, dimensions of Fall and Spring.

Thanks Karl.

Bloom Parade

Maybe life doesn't get any better than this, or any worse, and what we get is just what we're willing to find: small wonders, where they grow.

—Barbara Kingsolver

One I found early morning, late May, pulling out for my run at Mingus' track.

The march of the tree blossoms.
Majestic magenta bloomlets
on the newly surfaced
raven black carpet
that meets my drive.
I shift out of reverse.
Into their path.
Wind and wiley weather
in a strange unstable spring
have shorn them from their heights,
now send them toppling, tumbling
over and over
flashing fireworks
pulsing purples
rushing at my exiting machine.
No fields in sight
to compost in,

they give themselves
to *me.*

And now to you,
as I prolong their life,
in me,
and on this page.

And how strong the urge
to never lose a thing,
especially those
we deem as precious,
even as all wisdom teachers
whisper in our ear:
Kiss it as it flies.[7]

Joe Wise

Up, Up and Away

A prompt in writer's group, our first zoom during the Corona Virus Pandemic. We gave ourselves 15 minutes.

"Wouldn't you like to ride…?"

That's the post Covid verse. In the whole picture of my journey, it reminds me that on my path for greater and wider awarenesses of Truth—what is True about you and me and the world—on that path, or even in that balloon, I can only be a limited teacher of myself. Others in the gondola, maybe in every other verse, seems to be a pretty good curriculum.

So starting next week, I'll "invite" certain…(well they'll be certain *people*, but I'm not certain who they'll *be* yet) I'll invite certain people into the gondola, on the sky trip, the perspective jaunt, the higher view.

First, and maybe last, I think I'll ask J.T., James Taylor. After we're airborne I'll ask him if he knows "Up, Up, and Away."[8]

"I don't know that dimension. But I have been up on a roof. And I've seen fire and I've seen rain. I've got a friend, and I've seen times when I couldn't find one. And in the end I find the 'Secret O' Life'[9] is…well…'it's just a lovely ride.'"

Maybe then, I'll ask Art Garfunkel. Who wouldn't want to ride with a man who titled his autobiography, *What Is It All But Luminous?* Up, up, and away.

The Covid (19) and the Elder (80)

A writer. Sheltering in place. I get to go to work. And do what I do.

Corona Virus
They don't get it
Our petunias and pansies
They just don't get it
Don't get this dis-ease
They just keep on
Flourishing
Flora-ling
Broad casting beauty
By day
And by
Even night.
Rampant coloring
An eye-full
A soul-full.

Teach me your ways
Great groundlings
Help me not fear
In my autumn days
My expiration date
My date with dust

And ash—
And only *Be*
Full on *Be*
The whole unknown while.

Outbreak

This morning, as we were coming out of our meditation, Maleita looked at me and said, "What if *kindness* was the Corona Virus?

"And we all began to say, who were you in contact with? Who was *kind* to you? What happened? Why weren't they wearing the usual protective gear? To keep this from happening? Were there no 'indifference' masks? No 'wariness' gowns?"

If this radical no-fear substitute for weapons and safety is not eradicated swiftly, this will be the most infectious and unstoppable pandemic the world has ever known.

So far, I'm testing positive.

★   ★   ★   ★

And in Tibetan news, we hear His Holiness, the Dalai Lama, has blissed out, *really* out, like to another universe. Says he wants to be an intergalactic carrier.

March 1st

Spring is not here yet.
Not officially.
But apparently Cottonwood
here in Arizona
didn't get the memo.

She's already decking
herself out with
strawberry bloomin'
ice cream cones
to line her colorless
walkways and streets.
A vanilla one there
standing next to
the expectant naked
Sycamore.

Bushes too, yawning,
coming to bud
coming to life
even as they
come *from* Life
to my life.
Same Life,
even and especially

in the healthy
and virulent "weeds"
that I proclaim
as such
and uproot them
from my back yard's
scattering of
granite gravel.

Eckhart Tolle's aphorism
for today:
*A flower loves it
when you
see them.*

Today, is my
first March 1st
to know it is also
Compliment Day.

*God sleeps in stones
Stirs in plants
Dreams in animals
Awakens in humans.*

And so I choose
as *Awakener*
to see and bless and
be blessed by
the beauty of the
Stirrers,
even and especially
the healthy virulents,
the "weeds."

For as surely
as I compliment you
in your surging
unstoppable
stems and blades
and deep Verde hues
while I pull you
from our Mother,
we are
complementing
each other in
this Love-what-is world
we call Earth.

Hello Life.

Henny Penny

Please don't scare me any more than I am…scared.

I'm already knee deep in Covid and weeks deep in surrendering March Madness, *all* sports really, mine and others I watch, like the Kentucky Derby,[10] letting go of societal mixing, haircuts, Sunday gatherings, my own presentation of my writings and music and art, of going where everybody knows my name. With a naked breathing face.

And now, NPR's *Star Date* chooses today, the seventh of May, to feature, "Satellite Debris." Like there are kazillions of them and when they die they fall into the atmosphere and not everything burns up—*and* so far, "only 6 humans have been injured." I guess that's good news for all of us, except the six, who I'm sure didn't want to be exceptional, at least not like that.

But this is a game that has no clock, no finite number of innings. We're all still in there. How big would the piece have to be to kill me? A well placed screw or bolt could surely take me out.

But, if the *moon*, in its entirety, would fall and hit my eye, that would be different. That's ok. That's *amoré*.[11]

So, I'm rootin' for the *big* hit. The world can always use some more *amoré*. For you. For me. For itself.

Oh, and pizza.

And if there's a moose out there that took one for me, I'd sure like to pay my respects.

Our Pandemic/Systemic Racism

This remains my favorite account of creation. It is Zora Neal Hurston's.

> "When God had made the Man,
> He made him out of stuff
> that sung all the time and glittered
> all over. Then after that
> some angels got jealous and
> chopped him into millions of pieces,
> but still he glittered and hummed.
> So they beat him down to
> nothing but sparks,
> but each little spark
> had a shine and a song.
> So they covered each one over
> with mud. And the lonesomeness
> in the sparks make them
> hunt for one another,
> but the mud is
> deaf and dumb."

Our pandemic,
nationless, genderless,
classless, raceless.

A democratic dis-ease
with democratic responders
and so many possibilities
for awakenings.

Hope Springs

Hope springs green
In a season of code blue

Released from my cloister
For these precious minutes
I run the loop at Windmill Park

Hope springs cool
In the high desert sun
In the fresh morning dew

Hope springs maskless
In the arbor of solitude.

Hope springs yellow
In the surge of wild daisies
The flutter of Monarchs

Hope springs red
In my blood
Crimson, concealed
Life upon life
Mile after mile
Coursing its course
Vein after vein

Capillary, corpuscle
Thrumming and through-ing
Life after life
Hope springs…
Well…
Eternal.

Kadeetz

What's in a Name?

"Tony Bellucci."

"Tony what?"

"Tony *Bellucci*," isn't that a *great* name?"

He was running down the roster of his team-mates his high school was fielding this season. His baseball buddies. Most of the rest, all had nicknames. Tony's was too magnificent to fool with. *He,* went by "Johnny," and we were the two "maintenance men" who were getting this grade school in the west end of Louisville, all spiffed up for fall opening. I was home from seminary/college for the summer.

"Can't you just hear the announcer saying, 'And now, pitching for Flaget High, a senior from deep in the West End, Tony-y-y Bellucci-i?'" From my Latin immersion in school I open his surname—Bel-lucci—"Beautiful light." I decided sometime that day to name my newest treasure, my guitar, after him. I wanted, with its help, its tone, to cast beautiful light on whoever would hear "us." *Its* nickname became, "Tone-y." (It's still the one I go to, when I play for me.)

"This floor, is looking *good*," he proclaims loudly as we run the buffers over the newly waxed basement tile in the school cafeteria and all-purpose room. Machines we would turn off sometimes, mid-job, to listen to and take in a new song, from the radio station we had put up on the room's speakers. "*Sally, don't you go-o...don't you go downtown...Sally go 'round the roses...roses they won't hurt you...*"[12]

(ethereal vocals and counsel over a punchy straight-up rock riff). We both first heard The Beatles in this room.

★　★　★

It started with "Monjunior." Johnny's nickname for Right Reverend Monsignor Edward Van Bogart, our boss. Mon*junior*, easy enough to morph from Mon*signor*. Then it traveled through a couple more iterations, till it arrived somehow at Mon-ika-deetz—Kadeetz for short. It softened any stiffness or distance in the hierarchy of our relationship with our employer. Though he seemed to have a somewhat awkward time relating to most adults, and a frequently gruff exterior, his actual interactions with *us* always balanced out with care, and demonstrated love. I came to see a shyness in him. I worked many summers for him.

He fostered me in every way he could. He trusted me. When I was let go by a school of theology, still on my way to the priesthood, he gave me a room at the rectory, a job teaching at the grade school in the a.m. and janitor work in the afternoon. The room was for naps and study, as I was also going full time grad school at night. I was 24. I don't remember getting tired.

One afternoon, after lunch, he asked me if I would drive him downtown. I said, "Sure." He was going to a Catholic book and supply store to get a gift for his sister. As we walked in the store, immediately off to the left I see on an eye-level book shelf, Karl Rahner had released (in translation) volume 2 of his *Theological Investigations*. I lit up. "Oh look!"

"Uhp-hup, you don't want to be reading any of that nonsense, he's a heretic!" he barked. I wasn't surprised. Monsignor (I've never called him by his nickname and I won't here—only with Johnny or my cousin Maggie who Johnny was going with)—Monsignor, had studied *his* theology in Innsbruck, Austria at Collegium Canisianum, the very school where Rahner *taught*. He had *classes* with him! One of my heroes, one of a bevy of them just then. Pierre Teilhard de Chardin. Hans Küng. Edward Schillebeeckx. Their names were magic. It was the early 60's and things were shifting in the monolithic R.C. Church. To me, it felt like oxygen. I also still wanted to be a priest.

Monsignor got a rosary and a prayer book for his sister. Three days later, Rahner's *Investigations* appeared on my desk at the rectory. This characterized our relationship as clearly as anything else. He didn't "believe" in hardly anything I did, but he believed in *me*. He was lobbying the Archbishop to get me into another seminary.

Meanwhile, Christmas season came 'round. And as usual Monsignor (that is Johnny and I) started to get the church interior clean and bright, while rehearsals began for Midnight Mass. I was beginning to lead the community in singing the "new"/old English hymns, after the Vatican decided to go vernacular. So, he knew I could sing. And one afternoon, as I'm mopping the sanctuary, he ambled into the church and said he wondered if I could do something for him. His posture was everything but looking down and shuffling his feet. "Could you...would you...take your guitar...that guitar thing[13]...for the Midnight Mass...could you take it and play...and sing "Stille Nacht?"

Of course I could. It felt like something I could do for him, I *uniquely*, could do for him. After the years of long and wide support, care, and love he had given me. I felt like the child he never had, giving him something he couldn't give himself. *And*, he had shown me a vulnerable part of himself in the asking.

I had often, over the years, heard him coming down the school's echo-y empty halls of summer, toward the room I or we were cleaning, singing or humming, *"Muss I denn...muss i den...zu-um städtele hinaus...städtele hinaus...'cause I don't have a wooden heart."*[14] He loved German, he was fluent in it.[15] I assumed he'd been raised in it. Rahner's *Investigations* were written in German. He loved German-speaking Austria, especially Innsbruck, home of his alma mater, so when he asked me to sing "Stille Nacht" (Silent Night) I now wish I had learned it in German. Decades later I recorded it for my Christmas album, with verse one in German. Inside I dedicated it to him. It's my favorite (of all my recordings) vocal. By then he had long since passed, but when he asked, I now assume he knew the song's birth. The broken organ. The knee-deep-in-Advent, desperate choirmaster, Joseph Mohr. His Christmas poem. Remembering he had a guitar. Tapping his musician/composer friend, Franz Gruber. (Both from *Austria!*). And the boys' choir results.

What *I* did *this* Christmas, was to unwittingly duplicate most all of this narrative. I decided to also set four other texts intended for choir only (voices and guitar). He said ok, without hearing them. The experience the community had, including "their" sung parts, affirmed the assumption I had made, which was, instrumentation, or language, or newness of composition, had no bearing on the ability of all three to help us engage the unseen, embrace the mystical, stand in simple awe. The feedback was immediate and warm and full. It was a major "moment" in the unfoldment of what I would do with my young life's energy.

Johnny and I were already singing together in a group we had formed (with cousins and friends) calling ourselves the J.T. Singers, the J.T. part of which, as far as I know, is still a "mystery."[16]

There was no "mystery" around the folk music explosion of the early 60s. Pete Seeger had picked up the mantle with and after Woody Guthrie. Alan Lomax roamed the mountains seeking music and songs known only to the mountaineers. The (Francis James) Child collection, *The English and Scottish Popular Ballads*, in five volumes, was opened and sung. The Newport Folk Festival in Rhode Island ferreted out many African American players, writers, and singers, mostly from the South, who added and *were adding* to the seminal skeins of the fast looming quilt that was evolving, spinning out, in the U.S., flowering most famously with Robert Zimmerman (Bob Dylan) Joan Baez, and Peter Paul and Mary.

Johnny and I had been able to go to Newport (to see and hear and meet so many of my "other" heroes), traveling with scant funds and a generous friend who had a Nash Rambler, the folding seats of which made into our nightly motel room (for 3!). Every single night resulted in a last minute almost-asleep ploy for some limb to end up unwedged. Prolonging a final outcome (sleep) mostly by the inability of any of us to suppress laughter after somebody's successful maneuver. A time of great innocence. And hope. And open vistas everywhere.

All of it crashed for me, with Johnny's death.[17] At age 19. From a sled accident. A rusty runner stabbed through his thigh. Emergency miss-read the wound and didn't cauterize it deeply enough. He died, even with all his shots, of tetanus. I have loved no soul more than his.

Monsignor did the ceremonies and buried him, in shock, with love, and, like all of us who knew him, with a deep admiration of his brief life. Then added a stained glass window to the church, with his likeness.

I continued to clean the church. And his window.

I believe he helped resurrect me out of my grief.[18]

The singing group kept going. I began to sing solo. I began to write songs. Spiritual songs, for the "people," who were just coming out of song-silence, with a new R.C. agenda, and their own language.

★   ★   ★

Monsignor got me back into another seminary. I was there two weeks. Then called into the rector's office and told I was dismissed. "Why?"

"We don't give reasons to underlings."

Monsignor figured it out. After I came home, again. He said, "They opened your letter to me and re-sealed it." He had written me and asked, *how was the new seminary?* I had written in response, something like, *it's not a good place to train for maturity, much less for the priesthood.* The rector was later removed and committed to a mental facility.

I am back home. Dealing with another "rejection."[19] Wondering where I might fit. The "real" me. Monsignor re-hires me. Before I could ask. About a week into my work, cleaning a classroom, after school, I hear him clicking down the hall, singing a folk song popular *on the radio(!).* "Michael, row the boat ashore...milk and honey *on the other side...chills the body but not the soul."* He came in, made some comments on a couple of things to do in the room that were obvious and I had done a thousand times, then almost surreptitiously, certainly awkwardly, pressed a small folded piece of paper into my hand, and left abruptly. I stood, unsure of anything that had just happened, and of anything else that *might*—I stood for some time, then opened the paper.

"All things work unto good, for those who love the Lord."[20]

★ ★ ★

I signed up to study theology on my own at Catholic University in D.C. There was a department there that welcomed all my favorite thinkers, some of whom I got to *meet* and hear at Notre Dame, during an international theological conference held there. My new friends in D.C. had a car. We drove there. Again, I felt "at home" with these outliers.

In what I could only believe was a deep mercy on the part of the Universe and its Creator, I re-connected with John Grenough, still a priest then, at Johnny's wake. And with him, at his request, gave a retreat, and through him met Maleita. My Johnny, my son, has always called him "our founder." I also believe another Johnny played a role in it all.

Monsignor married us, or better, witnessed our marriage. The church I had cleaned for years was full and loud with new folk-sounding songs. Johnny's window shined bright. Monsignor preached on "Divorce." I was not surprised. I smiled. It's part of "who he is" in this incarnation. It didn't dampen us at all. I basically only saw Maleita that day. The school basement housed our reception, with my brother Denny's garage band. I/we were off. Launched.

Not too long after, we buried Monsignor. I got to see him in the hospital. The funeral Mass was at the church building we had both looked after. It was attended mostly by priests. To me it was terribly "Churchy." The tone was stiff and hierarchical and other-worldly, in the worst sense.

There was no recounting of the delight he took in taking all the servers, after weeks of rehearsals and some big ceremony, like Holy Saturday—taking us all to some restaurant we could never afford or even knew about, and watching us discover a shrimp cocktail, or a cut of meat we never knew. Treating us all with whatever dessert we could think of. Or the way he walked with me one evening through the neighborhood, now integrating and integrated, and lamenting, "we are bringing too little too late here." Or the time he was taking me to Mammoth Cave, driving me there, before my license as a driver, and I asked him if he ever wanted to be a bishop? There was an opening in the diocese. And he blushed, softened, and said with almost a smile, "No…no, not me." Shocked in part I believe, to be asked a personal question by one as young as me—or maybe by anyone. I expect he knew I thought he'd make a good one. He'd already worked at the chancery, in an office close to the bishop. He was the head of the marriages department and continued that work remotely at our parish. He was relentless as a barrister for the couple vs. the Church. As a part-time resident at the rectory I often heard, through closed doors, the heat and tenor of his arguments with downtown, the higher ups in the chancery, punctuated sometimes with a vigorous, slamming hang-up. A closet champion of love, for all who professed it.

As with Johnny, when he was buried, I watched alone from behind a tree. I was too afraid of what might happen with my grief. Or of somebody, especially somebody who didn't know me well, being jovial with me. Or of someone who *did* know me well, trying to "fix" my sadness. I felt I knew him uniquely, as a man who didn't have a "wooden heart."[21] His gruffness would say otherwise. And later I surmised he felt he had to look that way. Together and in charge. Maybe all his life.

A complex man, in a job that hamstrung many. Dehumanized many. His shield was gruffness. I was given a unique view through it.

I trust he found, the "milk and honey on the other side." And that all things worked unto good. And he could lay down his shield.[22] And say hello to Johnny, both in their Beautiful Light.

Prayers—Answered

Yes.

Not now.

I have something
better for you.

I Can't Complain

"I can't complain." Of course you can. And if you love yourself and have a friend, you will. And it'll be good for *both* of us. It'll lighten your load and make *me* feel less alone. More companioned.

Everybody needs what they need. That being said (a new substitute for "but" that's longer than "and") that being said, I have already run out of a need for unrelenting "upness" in anybody, including myself.

I allow myself, and others, occasions for faking it till I'm/we're making it, *but* (it's ba..a.ack) I prefer to shoot for a high percentage of being where I truly am at the time. I don't level off at Tony the Tiger. He's a kind of thrice in a lifetime benchmark, arrival...hope? One, when we have our first slug of milk. Two, when we find a friend. And three, a grandchild.[23] The rest is pretty wavy on a graph. With a tendency to dip a lot as we age. There is no better time to have a friend than elderhood. We have so much more to complain about.

To complain. Literally to be plain with. Not ornate. Not coating, sugar or otherwise. Straight on. This is where I am. This is me, now. Not a tactic for *convincing* you of anything, or *attempting to* over and over. This is sailing right past the buoy markers that say "embarrassment zone" or "pettiness just ahead." This is, after all, a friend, or may become one with this risky, brave-even sharing.

"Tried and true" becomes a part of the picture only with ongoing waves of disclosure. And share backs. Holding space for, sanctioning as it were, the possibility to say with great feeling, "I just want to strangle...(fill in the blank)...right now. Right this minute," and not precipitate the reach for a phone or a run out of the room. Whoever's turn it is to listen, to really *hear*, is given the gift of trust, and likely spontaneous felt empathy for the pain a friend is in. It has nothing to do with agreeing or disagreeing. Or even having an opinion. Stay with me. I won't ask you to be strong with me. Or "figure me out." Or, god forbid, try to "fix me."

A friend invites us, with or without words, to lay down the "I should be over this" mantle at the door. *She* knows I'm the only one who can say "that's enough." *He* is reminded of his own stubborn or frozen forgiveness trigger. And in the end it *is* about forgiveness. Forgiving *him* for being unconscious. Forgiving *her* for blind need. Forgiving me for being human. Forgiving the world for being the world.

★　★　★

There are stages of "complain" where "blame" masquerades as or truly believes *it is* "complain." Or being plain with. It lasts till it doesn't. Just like "victim" lasts until *it* doesn't. Though uncomfortable to be with, efforts to skip these stages seem to prolong the suffering. Being plain with *ourselves*, and with all of our feelings and motivations, *is* the goal and the liberator. The *jail* is fierce, because it looks so much like freedom. If it's your fault, I'm still "in control," and all I have to do is get *you* or *it* to change. Way easier. And way more familiar, since by definition we haven't picked up *our* responsibilities and our *powers* in this (fill in the blank) arena yet.

★　★　★

Why is it so easy to be hard on somebody else for acting out of his or her own set of thoughts and assessments? I am beginning to see more clearly when the opposite, a compassion, arises in me, it's either because I think "I'm above this" or it arises as "I've *done* this" or "I *could* have." *Its* gift: the possibility of recognizing the latter, "I did" or "could have" is the *connecting* one. The one without the distance.

I *can* complain. And I do. Maybe not enough.

★　　★　　★

All this reminds me of Daniel Ladinsky's placement of this poem in his *A Year with Hafiz*,[24] the Persian poet and mystic, on *my* birthday in August.

> *It is the nature of this world*
> *to share with you*
> *Its burden.*
> *And it is my nature*
> *To remove it*
> *From your back.*

Stay at Home

Notes from the Shelter

If you're lucky
you have known
someone
who can bring "home"
to any room.
When you are
with them
you might cry
out of a primal
remembrance of "home."
Who you were
before you were
some body.
Before you had
to qualify with *you*
if not with *them*,
to feel welcome.
At ease.

Beyond and underneath
dis-ease.
The most natural
of all "states,"
your united states,
Home.

Coming Out of Covid

Onward.
And outward?
Inward?
Upward?
Down…
Back…
Forw…
???

All the above.

How to Watch a U of K Game

This one comes from writing group. We write and share in session. Assignment by today's leader: "Blog on something you're good at. Even an expert in. Twenty minutes." A "how to," with five points, or bullets. (In my case "points" and "bullets" became relevant in the extreme.)

As most of you know, I'm a huge, no, obsessively humongous fan of the University of Kentucky's basketball team. In 1948 I wrote to, and got answers from (these were times when players got their mail) every single one of the "Fabulous Five." Alex Groza, Ralph Beard, Wah Wah Jones (did he also play Trumpet?), Cliff Barker,[25] and Kenny Rollins. Besides their national championship that year, they, as a group became basically the USA's team (*with* coach Rupp) in the Summer Olympics. With similar, "golden," results.

I have listened to (before TV) and/or watched (some "live") pretty much every game they've played since. I have a friend, Eric, in (or near) Kentucky (now over the river, in another, to be unnamed, basketball state) I call before and after the game. Before I moved to Arizona, from Louisville (I know, U of L, tough choice) I watched every single Kentucky game at his house, with him and Margie, yelling, cheering, moping—whatever was called for.

Now, mostly alone (Maleita in and out, or *sits* for big games—she still has the capacity to differentiate. I lost that in about...1952)... now, mostly alone, I watch.[26]

These are my Five Essentials:

1) Make sure there are no young children in the house—I don't want to contribute to an expanded vocabulary that may not serve them well in a useful life.

2) Make sure my 77 year old bladder won't call for attention till at least half-time.

3) A pre-game talk-myself-down regarding near-sighted or otherwise handicapped officials.

4) Update my living will. And in perhaps a related matter...

5) Don't have a firearm within reach.

These may (seem to) be pretty self-evident words of wisdom (*maxims*, if you will) but they've seen me through twenty hundred and forty one games without incident. Though, indeed, *you* may find *you* need more *severe measures*, depending on your current health, and untreated level of addiction.[27]

So, buckle up. Good luck. And Go-o-O CATS!

Love, Synthia

I'm including this piece, allowing myself this shameless indulgence, for no other reason than "I can." I could invoke "destiny" and set forth all manner of lofty considerations. But the simple truth is, I am a basketball freak, lover, junkie, enthusiast, addict, fan. No, don't pick one. They're all legit.

I am, also, one who was *born* the same year as the NCAA Tournament. One month before, that season's practices and games began. Long before "One Shining Moment,"[28] though I certainly *was that* for *me* and (I assumed for) my family. *And* I played on my first school team (6th grade) the year Converse created and released to schools the original, first edition (though I doubt they had any idea this was *any* edition at the time) Chuck Taylor, All-Star, canvas, high-top (that is over-the-ankle) athletic shoe.[29] Designed specifically for indoor wooden basketball courts. Never knew who ole "Chuck" was, but I bet he would turn over in his Naismith peach-crate-basket coffin, if he could see the casual surfaces and "profane" "courts" his high tops trod today. In this christening year, I became the only kid in my family with an "extra" pair of shoes, to be worn of course, only on the specified surfaces. This, even though I never played for or at a school, for *any* team, that *had* a gym, until my second graduate school, at age 26. It never occurred to me that we never had the benefit of having home games. I was just excited to play in a gym. Anybody's. Any time.

Those "Chucks" stayed on the shelf for all my practices, on school grounds or public parks. Honored by me, the way my parents had honored my early hoops affliction, with their bestowal. They had also offered me guitar lessons at about this time, but I was already committed. To another kind of "string music."[30]

I was also playing simultaneously for Eagle Beak's team. His *basketball* team. His baseball team as well, the Sealtest Tigers, the sport he was most known for talent-scouting in, Pee Wee Reese[31] being one of his most famous finds. It was *something* to have him choose you and coach you. As for his name, Eagle Beak,[32] I always assumed it was because of his prominent proboscis (not to be confused with his *dominus vobiscum*). *And* it was the only thing I ever heard anybody call him. Kind of like "Superman." I never knew his Clark Kent name. Our basketball team, from all over the city, played only already existing school teams, some out of town (cool!) and only teams older than us. He told us it would make us better players. I wavered between believing that and that we were game fodder, juvenile Washington Generals to statewide teams with Sweet Georgia Brown theme-songs.[33] I loved it all.

Before "Chucks" and teams, I shot at nailed up alley boards and baskets, usually on garages, in my neighborhood. None were less than the (official) ten feet. My ball was always official size and weight. Big ball—ten feet. Was this all a secret ploy to get me to eat my Wheaties, "the breakfast of champions?" I hoped so, as the alternative was adults were far more nefarious than they appeared to be.

Tom, a man who worked for my Dad at American Tobacco Company, would sometimes come by and shoot with me in the alley. My Dad told me Tom always carried a basketball and a shovel in his car. He shot almost every day, even on snowy days in winter. I was impressed by my Dad, that he knew a guy like this. My Dad wasn't a "jock," but he used to play golf, and still went bowling. To me bowling, just like golf, had too many "accidents," things nobody could control. Some pins were more "lively" and all of them bounced so randomly. One more coat of paint or lacquer on that one and it would have been grazed and gone down. Too "iffy." Oh, and the ball was heavy. In later life I softened to golf and not only lost my disdain for the unpredictable, but began to in many instances, after my part was "done," pray for them.

The first gym I got to play in was only a ten block walk from home, and became "mine" one summer when I was allowed to go to a "Basketball Camp." I couldn't sleep there at night, but I would have. Mr. Varble was our instructor, and if not a deity, at least a Seraphim, as he had the keys to the kingdom. I learned how to shoot with a little more accuracy every day. How to guard with the fewest moves, when to dribble, when to not, and a holy host of passes. A lot of this already felt instinctual, but it was great to hear him, and watch him, and then have *our* go at it. *And* feel his desire for our betterment. As kids, as well as basketball acolytes. My favorite time of day that summer was after breakfast, all "Wheatied" up, setting out by myself, Chucks tied together and strung over my shoulder, like sideways saddlebags, walking lightly down the neighborhood sidewalks, looking neither left nor right, dead bound for heaven.

I had a purgatory's worth of struggle, learning to shoot an underhanded free throw. Knowing someday it would be part of a "real," not playground, game gave me all the petrol I needed to persist. Who knew that a son, Canyon, of a pro, Rick Barry, would resurrect this shot, and set a University of Florida school record, of 42 straight game makes, 17 years after the turn of *the millennium*. By the end of the camp, I had it. I lived through the underhand free throw, the two handed set shot off the chest, joined the jump shot revolution in my high school years, developed a short-guy (5'11") hook, and lived *into* the era of $495 footwear.[34] A Kardashian approach to the game if ever there was one.

As I write this there is yet another investigation into misdeeds in the college game. I don't want to, but I do accept that when we find a game we like and a lot of other people do too, we often enter into something other than play, and fair competition. I don't like it. I'm glad we eventually ferret it out. *And* I refuse to surrender my love and joy and acid reflux, all the sweat and enthusiasm I faithfully contribute to this sport, to "my" team, to all *my* shining moments and experiences, as a *fan*.

And so without further ado, or further a-*don't*, I proceed to the "letter," the missive, the document that all this was supposed to be a short preamble to...made a little bit longer now, in *this phrase*, in order to not end this sentence with a preposition. All games have rules. Even writing. All games can have fun. Or acid reflux. Or both.

Enjoy or groan to your heart's content.

The envelope please...

"Synthia" (Synthetic) Spalding
3 on 3 Layup Lane
Red Shirt, KY One plus one plus one plus one plus one

Gymnasium
222 Alley Oop Alley
Bounce Pass, Indiana 00002

August 11, 1989

Gymnasium
222 Alley Oop Lane
Bounce Pass, Indiana 00002

Dear Gym,

I *do* know you too well to call you Gymnasium. I almost called you "Gymmie." I miss you. Anytime I'm not with you. I so look forward to our time together. Our lunchtime rendezvous. I remember the first time I saw you—the afternoon sun setting you all aglow—and the fragrance I've come to know as only yours. I wasn't braced for what was about to happen.

You. You were so forward, you took me right off guard. It was intentional, wasn't it? I have had all I can handle rebounding, and re-centering myself. I've cried buckets and swished many a swizzle stick trying to let go of "Stadium," my first love. At first it was a tossup between you and "Sta." But with an able assist from my therapist, who pointed out I only dribbled and drooled as I talked about you, how offensive I was starting to see "Stadium" as, and how defensive I was about *you*, I am at last able to make the call. It's you Gym. I'll accept no substitutes.

My family is zoned out over this. My brother asked me if you gave me a base line. I told him it was just the converse. He says he'd be hard pressed if he only had 45 seconds to get it off.[35] I told him it was none of his business. Foul mouth. My mom. She is so naïve. She wanted to know if you made a pass at me. I told her *I* was doing the passing. And my Dad, all he wants to know, is your net worth.

They don't understand modern courting. They haven't a clue what the score is. Shall I tell them it's official? After all I'm in my third quarter...er...trimester. I sure hope he's official size and weight. I'll count on your coaching at Lamaz.

Your All American Sweetheart,

Synthia

No Sweat Synthia

P.S. Can we call our little free throw something other than Kareem? Already taken. And, too much pressure.

Hunkering

In the bleak Midwinter
I wear crocus clothes.

Bright yellow turtlenecks
A high desert bloom I am.

Never cared much for Winter
Yet Winter still cares for me.

With pace, and deprivation,
Hope challenges, and rest.

Within-ness.

David Linker

This is a family letter I sent to David's brothers and sisters, there were ten of them, when I was unable to go to his funeral. He was an integral part of so many of my early adulthood years. Among other activities, we shared working at our parish's church and school as maintenance men. I include it here as a tribute to his life.

Dear Bonnie, Brothers, and Sisters,

This letter is as close as I will get as a visit. I wish it could include more presence. Wish I could be in the rooms to hear all the facets of David that will be shared. Here are some of mine.

I better start with the war, so I can get uncloudy for the rest. I so admired his courage. I so hated the war, and Agent Orange, and the hideous things he "had" to do.

Now for the *clear* stuff. Some vintage David. Running the floor polishing machine in the breezeway at St. Ben's between the priests house and the church, and I walk in with more equipment from the school building, and see Mary—the Mother of God one—holding his cigarette between her first two fingers—outstretched to the world. He looks at me, "Hey…she's cool."

A devious plot against Ms. Shaughnessy, the organist. He undertook, in the choir loft, a multilayered furniture polish approach to having her skid off her bench when she slid in. "I know we won't see her, but we'll know it worked if she needs to grab the keys."

Pairing up to go get the Church's Christmas tree. I'm newly licensed and Monsignor lets me take his car. With the big trunk. David decides he should ride *with* the tree, in the trunk. The first traffic light I come to, the car behind me's driver bounds out of her car, runs up to my open window and says, "Is that a *body* in your trunk?" David, perhaps anticipating Halloween, through the small opening of the tied down trunk, was dangling his arm.

He never failed to bring delight to and out of Michelle, my daughter, his God-baby, in her early years. Comfortable with even the "wordless" ones. Finding common language and connection.

He was Batman, before Michael Keaton, for Maleita and me, one night down on Broadway at Fontaine House, our new home, when we couldn't, with just the two of us, get a bat to fly out of the house. The call went out. David showed up, and came up with the *strangest* ideas, I think now, just to see if we would *do* them—involving tennis rackets and mops, vocalizing, and something resembling military flanking...I'd love to have the video. I *do* have it in my heart. The bat flew out, I'm convinced, because he thought we were crazier than he was.

I was honored to have received and shared confidences with David and to have his spirit and voice wedded to mine in so many recording sessions. Being the "permanent" and widest way my songs would be shared. Giving him my practice tape. Never rehearsing. Breathing together. Timbre matched. Word-sound matched. Volume matched. Intent/meaning matched.

His greatest gift to me, and I'm sure to you all, was/is his Presence. When he was here, he was *here*. When he was with me he was *with* me.

I count on that remaining true. For the next time.

Love,
Joe

The Cycle

Fall is just
part of the cycle
no ender of things
no more than ole spring
who
calls to a halt
the naked
and free branch
the twig in the buff
the stem in the rough
the part to remember
is cycle
not ender.

Browning

This piece was as difficult to write as it was to experience. The thirty or so years between helped with perspective, with the acquisition of the tools to process the "events" herein, and with the capacity to place all this where it fit, into the arc of my overall story, this overall earth life. So far.

If you are reading this as a stand-alone piece and are new to my writings it would be helpful to know what came before, that may have given so much weight to these brief (calendar-wise) three days in a life.

I come at this from an Irish/Catholic "tribe." From a walk-to-church Catholic neighborhood. From an entire, school-wise, education (K through four degrees) at Catholic schools and universities, ten and one half years of which were in Catholic seminaries.

I come to this as a coming-of-age thinker, in the early sixties, dropped from the seminaries as too progressive, resonating with new visions of a community of followers of Jesus' Way, with much more inclusion, and equality, de-institutionalizing spirituality and fostering direct "contact" with the divine, through the sacraments of everyday life. As with Martin Luther and John Wesley, I called upon music and song, lyric and melody as a prime language.

I come to this with almost twenty five years of spreading and affirming, by individual invitations, this belief and knowledge of a living divine now-Presence, throughout the English speaking world, mostly to Catholics, but to many other institutions and communities as well. I saw no line between secular and sacred. No divine absence in anything.

I come to this feeling like Johnny Appleseed and Hans Christian Andersen, spreading joy and hope and comfort.

Browning appeared on my calendar, at a time when the institutions, so hopefully opening to some things new, were backlashing, and I was in trouble with alcohol. I was sober. But freshly so.

My therapist said he had never seen someone have so long a "ride" like mine, and that "I knew too much" (about the Roman Catholic Church).

Browning, Montana.

The beginning of the end.

Browning, Montana. The land of the Blackfoot. The home of the Blackfoot. Actually, neither. Not a chosen home. It would be some other place. And no "owned" land. Until we second-comers "made it so." *Who could* own *the land?* was the question these stewards asked.

On this land, with these people, I began at some level knowing I could not be true to myself and continue the work I was doing. This clarity registered only as pervasive pain, at the time.

I had the gift of a companion on this trip. John, my friend and travel buddy from Nashville. I couldn't wait to share him and me with these people. "Give something back" was part of a not-so-subconscious text for me here.

As it came down, all the real gift-giving was *to me.* Though I recognized so little of it as gift, at the time.

Mike Little Dog, our host, met us at the airport in Great falls and drove us through a gorgeous patch of Big Sky Country toward Browning. As soon as we were settled in the van and on the open road, I asked him where he got the name "Mike." He said the priests who came years ago had everybody get a Christian name and cut their hair. It was like I had been surprised by a spear to my chest. It literally hurt to have him say this. With what turned out to be a level of acceptance and maturity and faith that eclipsed my tenuous foothold on a mid-life "self."

We pulled into Browning. Lots of dust in the air. Lots of men and women leaning forward in the wind to walk. Lots of men not sober enough to walk. I am in the early stages of being without *my* bottled self-medication for pain.

The town is small. Non-descript. Not many visible places of business. I comment on this. He says the government doesn't allow them to have a bank in town. He drives to the next town for that. One off the *res*.[36] I am gradually beginning an effective emotional brown out. I am shutting down my feeling life, as completely as I can, to "get through," "function" well enough to deliver my (still-perceived) gift. Like the numbness of a cut, until the body/mind is ready to cope with a wound, my psyche was producing shell, and movement through life, much like a turtle.

It "begins" here, where I am becoming profoundly ashamed to be Christian/Catholic *and* "American." I know I personally did not do this "thing" to these already-here people, both *now* and *then*, but it *felt* like it. Everything in me wanted to say, "We were having a bad day." A bad year. A bad century. Or two… Anything I *could* say felt so inadequate, so superficial, so…late. The only authentic response for me would have been wordless weeping. For them, for me. What I hadn't called out in myself. What "my people" had done, were doing to my "no-less-people." What I was doing to my*self*. My Self. As them. As me.

Mike little Dog took us to the parish priest's residence. The pastor was away for a few days, and John and I would stay there. I can't remember what John or I did or said when Mike Little Dog left. I remember feeling shell-shocked and almost afraid to look at, or say anything to, anybody, for fear I would melt completely and uselessly down. I think we just stayed in our own "now," which was usually warm, natural, curious and/or funny. This was full on neutral for me.

Memories of this trip are sketchy and strobe-like. Men, mostly inebriated, coming to the front door asking for food or money. Sitting at Mike Little Dog's family table with his immediate "tribe," and how everyday welcoming the company was, how full of care the meal unfolded with, how far away I felt from it all. I have no idea whether I wore a happy face, guilty face, or blank face at that table.

I *do* remember, vividly, my asking Mike Little Dog, after the meal, what he did. And his reply being, "I help my people understand and fill out U.S. government papers." I had meant, what did he do to get *through* this life. *His* current way of life. A day in this life. I left out how utterly awed I was by his balance, energy, commitment, and his natural-as-flow-to-a-river selflessness.

His answer was to lead me toward the back of his house. To a room that looked like a closet. He opened the door. "The priest lets me bring the Blessed Sacrament home to this altar. I am here in the morning from 4:00 until 6:00." A small windowless room with a chair, a kneeler, an end table with candles, and the consecrated Wafer from the Mass.

He was finding solace and strength, in the silence, via the Roman Catholic version, along with its accoutrements, of Jesus' "Way."[37] The same version *I* saw as, more than subtly, in policy, pronouncements and personnel, hierarch-ing people, with strong emphasis on the lower echelons being occupied by lay people in general, with women, in particular, being at the bottom of the bottom category.

Then there was our concert. A Sunday afternoon concert, held in, no doubt, the most beautiful room in Browning. A kind of theatre/meeting place framed by, and appointed with all log pole and plank timber of endlessly warm and interesting burl and vein. It stood in stark contrast to the dusty dying edifices all around it. The rest is blurry in my recall. Three sticks in my mind, but maybe as many as five people came to the concert. I sang for them. I sang my best for them. Pah-rump pum pum pum. At least I hope, through my distractions, I did. I'm confident John played his finest. I was never not somewhere beyond proud to be staged with him. I mostly hoped Little Dog (I can't use his Christian name any more) got *something* from me, from us. Anything.

He didn't (wonderfully) apologize for the size of the crowd. Instead he said he had one more gift to give *us*. A trip to and a night's stay for just us two in Glacier National Park. On the lake. It didn't used to be a trip. It used to be home to his people, the whole Glacial National Park area. "Our" people decided they could have Browning instead. The most barren part of "home." Blown into dust by the Mountain's natural, unending, relentless air current. He told us, without any irony, how you could tell the (lean into the wind)

Browning man in Billings or Helena: "He falls down." It could have been an alcohol–impairment reference, but it wasn't. Not from Little Dog.

It seems some snippet of heart or perhaps the cleverness of some attorney aligned with the Blackfoot resulted in the granting of a small parcel, extremely small, in the Park, on (I believe) St. Mary Lake. The Blackfoot had built a cabin there, and it was to be a night's luxury for Little Dog's guests. As cold as I/we were (it *was* winter or its fringe) and as frayed as *I* was, every ounce of me cried out for home in Kentucky, in any place of familiarity. Anywhere. *And* there was no way I/we were going to refuse this gift, this honor. He played his best for us.

I can't remember if we built a fire that night to warm the cabin. I remember shivering, probably from more than cold. The lone picture/photo I have of this trip is of John, in the cabin, the following morning, sitting in a chair, engulfed in and thoroughly tented by, a beautiful hand-loomed blanket, willing the chill away. We walked out only once and briefly. To see the lake. That and the Park's beauty fell on my open, blind eyes. My sheltered and shut down heart.

Little Dog came for us that afternoon. He took us to Great Falls and had to return to his people. Our flight wasn't till morning, so he put us up in an airport motel. And paid us. For our "work." In cash. Not allowed a checking account!

As soon as he left, I looked at John, and said, "I can't keep this." He said, "I can't either." I waited till I thought Little Dog might be home[38] and called him. I said, "John and I would like to return this money to you. Could you receive it?" He said, "I can." Simply. It was such a relief. I felt so much in "debt" to him, to his people. For obvious, as well as un-nameable reasons. I sent a money order as soon as I got home.

Home? What is home? *Where* is it? I was coming unmoored from so many docks I had called by this name. So many *ports* I returned to, now felt foreign, unfamiliar, cold. Though I never thought Maleita would be one such, I "knew" the shape of our relationship would be up for change, in some (as yet to be determined) dramatic ways.

If I left this work, which was becoming more and more toxic to me, I wouldn't know who I'd be, I wouldn't know how to explain it to anybody right now, even to myself. I would lose the "fame," the image of me I'd formed by how I was treated. I would lose the money, the income. What would I do? I had no second career in mind or in the wings. What could I do that wouldn't turn my lights out?

What could I tell my "fans," people who I'd come to know and been supported by for over two decades? All around the world. Many of whom told me how comforted and encouraged they were in their faith and lives by my work and presence.

It slowly became clearer to me I was so caught up in my "good fight" against the institutions of religion, mainly Roman Catholicism and all its narrowness, I was losing *myself.* Three big pieces here, in more and more focus down the road. It was a *fight.* And I was losing. And losing *me.*

It was a fight. A much stronger "hidden" driver than I could/would allow myself to see. So much more of my motivation and energy than I could admit, was guided by and given to *pushing against* the status quo, the, to me, short-sighted behemoth headquartered in Rome, and any other dogma'd entity. Not *solely* (as I had told myself) offering a lot of fun, and fuller options, and other direct ways (no intermediaries) to a more personal connection to and with the Divine.

I was losing. By now the backlash from those unwilling to carry forward any more open inquiry initiated in the 60s was in full swing.

I was losing *me.* Including *my* open inquiry. For me.

Browning, an experience to unseat even the most resolute knight at the height of his skills, took me down. Hard. I had had much "soft," and years, decades of seeing the difference I could help foster in so many communities, championing personal spiritual authority, freedom, and growth.

Browning, the beginning of the end. And the beginning of the beginning. A restart. A monumental, even if its size became apparent to only me, restart.

Beginning with my disgorge of all things Browning at my weekly aftercare meeting at the treatment center. And having the 24-year-sober group leader calmly, clearly, and, I felt, lovingly, tell me, "I see how much pain this has caused you, but right now your 'Magnificent Obsession' is to do whatever you have to do to get and stay sober." I surrendered to this wisdom. I was teachable. I was unsure. Of almost everything. I was brave. I didn't know where that came from. I would find out. It was not separate from me/Me.

★   ★   ★

On the day I finished fashioning this piece, by hand, on paper, in the Cottonwood Library, I stood up from my writing table against one wall, gathered my tools and walked between the stacks opposite my station toward the far wall as my way out. The stacks were like blinders for my peripheral vision, leaving only my direct far-seeing focus in play. At eye level "coming" closer and closer to me was a portrait. Surely hung recently or maybe even while I was there *today.* I check the walls when I enter for new paintings, as a local artist coalition rotates pieces in and out. Closer. A reddish-brown face. Closer. A two dimensional bust. Closer. With feathers... Titled "Great American Indian."

★   ★   ★

I continued with some engagements, mostly concerts, after Browning, not fully sure yet what my "pain" meant. I had so much free floating anxiety at the time, I didn't want to let that alone, unexamined, be my reason for walking away from this work, this calling (?), this "life." I was at the threshold of a few years of interior work, allowing past hurts and personal traumas to surface, this time with *all* their *emotional* force and content, and engaging myself in the process of healing. Healing beginning only as I gave up inner insistence on a "cure." The future was a cloud, a dense fog, staying resolutely just in front of my every step. Becoming its own lesson.

★ ★ ★

The Sunday after this writing declared itself complete. I was heading off to do a "job" I was asked to do a while back in and for my spiritual community. Our service is at 10:30. Previous to that we have a half hour (9:30 to 10:00) set aside for silent communal meditation. I was on my way to be, what I had humorously dubbed, DMIC: Designated Meditator in Chief, the only physical requirements of which was being embodied, then sitting in a chair, facing the participants.

This takes place in a smallish, intimate, dancer's rehearsal/practice room, Studio B, just off the main building housing the service. Its intimacy is given an openness by a long, that is to say, wide floor to ceiling mirror, with attached hand bar for the dancers, all across the rear wall. This is only the second time we're in this new space, "home," allowing more time for our minsters and service leaders to do physical, mostly technical set up, checks, and tests, in the "big" room. I like this space for this.

During the coming-up-on 9 years I've been a member of this community, essentially since its inception, I've had the former and current minister invite me to talk, sing, read, or be the "platform person" (overall master of ceremonies) on Sunday. After almost 25 years of leading spiritual services, solo, or with a team, in just about every capacity, I could tell them (and me) *Thanks for asking.* And, *no.* Adding I want to be a member, a sit-with member, not an in-front-of-people member. To have my connections with people come clearly and only from my heart and current "place" and not "clouded" (by me or by them) in or by any ministry or role I may have. To be one among. *And* to *be* served. It is *my* turn. I want to "belong" in this new way.

I had had a 30 year break from being part of a spiritual community, as none I'd looked into felt like a fit. Then I met Bruce. A true companion. Open to all spiritual inquiry. As his *life.* Not his "job."

And now 9 months ago, a new leader and companion, Arvel. Open. Truth student. Long time spiritual "warrior," declaring himself as Celtic Indian, both in ancestry and soul. My wee percent Native American and most percent Irish, as well as so many life experiences and faith journey parallels, draw me in. I am also struck, moved and inspired by the "all in" commitment he and Kimberly, his wife, have made to this community, and beyond, a dynamic work in progress.

So here I am, when the volunteer coordinator asks me, agreeing to be the one who sits facing the ones who come to meditate. I see this as a presence with three dimensions. One, to be the primary "holder of the space" for the meditators. Mostly by going inward myself. Two, to contribute *to* and receive *from* this gathering of souls in the silence, in our beingness, as well as to radiate outward, world-wise, my/our communion with the Truth of who we are, and our connection with our Source, Spirit, God, Creator. And three (we are in descending order here) by my position and face, to let anybody who walks in, from the back, unsure, see in a moment, we are meditating here. In a group. Where two or three are gathered...

All the way to *this* Sunday, after my "visit," via my writing, to Browning. A few more than "two or three" are gathered. We enter the silence... I wear or carry nothing that tells me the time (since I was 18). I am feeling like it's a half an hour. In the "big" room, when we meditated there, the sound and light technician would slowly bring up the lights and fade in some peaceful wordless music, to signal the transition out of the meditative state. It's mine now to signal. I open my eyes and the clock on the back wall tells me it is a little past "time."

I do something I haven't done before. I look at the faces of each of us in silence. In this case all eyes are closed but mine. It is a beautiful thing. A "let's-put-up-three-tents" thing. A sweetness. A peace. A glow. Simultaneously I see in the big rear mirror, all the backs and me facing them, facing me. I tear up. A deep awareness floods me.

All the years I was in front of people, sought to be there, doing everything I could, usually as a solo leader, to help them be in touch with their spirits, their souls. Believing if I just did enough, or just the right things, the surrender they may have made to religion as institution, might be re-considered, and the clarity and truth of their own experience and their own spiritual authority might shine through. The intensity of these efforts, writing songs that messaged this, performing them, praying them, recording them, preparing retreats and workshops, leading liturgies and services... All this came rushing in on me. A large wave. Settling more and more, and then *completely*, in *ocean* me. Me *"doing"* nothing. Me, as a member. Me, not "leading" anything. Me, connected, communing with such willing participants. Not on any mainstage. Here, in Studio B. Readying ourselves to be led, in outer and inner invitations, to be led, invited, and companioned by a "Great American Indian." And a fine man. And a beautiful soul.

Pure gift.

What Remains

I gave up my career. Not my work.
I gave up my concept of my career
    and how it would look.
I continue to do the work I came here for.
        To awaken, more and more to the Truth
           of all Being.
Not to become more holy.
I/we are already as holy as we're going to get.
      That is to say—completely, irrevocably,
      effulgently, totally holy.
      As we were made.
And to share and teach about that.
To know more deeply how undivided
      and non-separated we are from God,
      from Self, within ourselves,
      from each other.

A Thing as Lovely

I think that I shall never see
A thing as lovely as a tree
Unless of course it would be me.

My branches old, more spindly now
A host of wrinkles grace my brow.
Each a testament to when and how

I opened up a part of me
To find the Truth inside of me
And let it out to speak of Thee

The maker of my soul and tree
And bird and bloom and ecstasy

We sing it daily you and me
The universe, and stars like me.

Picture of Myself as a Child / Me and Billy

This comes from a writer's workshop I conducted in conjunction with a reading I did at the Peregrine Book Company in Prescott, Arizona. The assignment was to let a favorite picture of yourself as a child come to you. I gave us 5 minutes to write a description, like a reporter, of the scene, and then 20 minutes to explore the "heart" of the photo/image in your then "voice."

I am about 10 or 11. Sitting under a rear porch overhang. My house and home on Date Street in Louisville. Sitting at a card table—across from me is Billy Huffman. We are playing cards. It is spring. Mom has some clothes on the line. I am in shorts, no shirt or shoes. Billy has short sleeves and long pants. My hair is pretty short. It is light. From the sun. I believe my Dad took this picture. It is black and white. I am smiling. Billy's back is to the camera, so I can't see his face right now. I *can* in the moment this was captured. I stay tan all year round. *Now* I'm *light* tanned.

★   ★   ★

Billy Huffman is my best buddy. He's also the only friend I have who comes to my house. I go to other people's houses. I think some of my friends are afraid of my Dad. He's not the same all the time. He changes when he drinks.

We don't do this much, me and Billy. Playing cards. We ride bikes a lot. And he lets me help him deliver papers. I love getting up early to go to his house and start the paper route. There's nobody bossing us. There's nobody *awake*. Our world. I don't get sleepy in school either. I like to go to his house. Billy's Mom is great and sometimes me and Billy sit and listen to baseball games with his Dad. His Mom and Dad stay the same all the time. I like that feeling. His Mom's a good baker too.

When we ride our bikes we go *way out* of our neighborhood. Downtown sometimes. Riding between the parked and moving cars, sometimes buses. We're both good at that. Sometimes we ride over the bridge into Indiana. We *never* tell our parents where we've been. It doesn't feel like a *bad* secret. It feels like a *good* secret.

We also sometimes get sent to sell chocolates for school—*during school time.* We stretch *that* as far as we can. Sometimes we get into trouble at school. Fun for us, but trouble for the teacher. One time a music chart on rollers got torn and they had a meeting of the whole school and before they asked who did this, they asked Billy and me if *we* did it. We didn't. But I felt like a good "bad guy" if I was even *suspected.*

I love that I don't have to take care of him. Mom and Dad, mostly Dad, want me to look out for the rest of my brothers and sisters. I take my brother to the Doctor and stuff. I was supposed to take care of my Mom while Dad was in the war. That felt strange. Good because I was "equal" to the big people. Bad because I had no idea what to do, and I didn't have much play time, or time for me. Billy is cool. He never asks me about my family. I wouldn't know what to tell him anyway.

7-29-2017

When I Meditate

When I meditate
I have
a Martha/Mary mind.

I *know* what
"choosing the better part" is,
but I'm usually
out in the kitchen,
"gettin' it done."

Finding My Way

75

Gallery 87

When Gallery 87 (on state highway 87) in Pine, Arizona had its grand opening in May of 2004, it featured Maleita and me as artists, gave our works the most space and prominence on its walls, and asked us to present something of our paths as visual artists. This was mine.

I began to draw, to see if I could. I could. I began to draw to see if I could make it look *exactly* like what I was drawing. I was close. I wasn't as close as Bob Burckel. In the seventh grade he drew a *White Fang* that could have gone in the book. Or *on* it.

I was better at basketball. I mostly wanted to do something to get people, especially my parents, amazed. I wasn't a great basketball player. I was an enthusiastic average player. Overall it seemed more fun than drawing and gave me a bigger release. I played on school teams, intramurals, and in leagues till I was 52.

The same community center I was playing ball at, at 52, was offering "adult drawing." Not feeling particularly adult at the time, but feeling like drawing, I took it. Drew upside down with Betty Edwards, as in *Drawing on the Right Side of the Brain*. I couldn't draw a hand, I told myself, but when I turned the Picasso line drawing in the book upside down, as she instructed, and drew the shapes between the fingers, I *could*. I had had a 40 year break. It came back. With juice.

My expressive energies for well over 20 years had gone into songwriting, recording, producing, performing. I was burning out on that. I took watercolor. I loved it. Lots of interaction between me and the paper. We *all* contributed. A lot like life.

My only other experience with color was with my coloring books in grade school. I stayed in the lines. I colored everything the "right" color. Who would want a purple Roy Rogers and a green Trigger?

I would, now. It would be ok. It might be fun. It might help me see things freshly, differently. I followed the same path I did in writing and basketball. I got the fundamentals down. Then I *played* with them, *fought* with them, *juggled* them, and in some blessed cases *forgot* them, as my own unique contribution began to flow through me.

This was a few years down the line. I began as I had left off. Drawing and painting as close to what I saw as I could. When I wanted to move past the realistic toward the abstract—not abstract in the sense of dry—but in the sense of juicy. What is the feeling here? What is the essence here? How do I interact with this subject on the inside? When I wanted to move *there*—it felt like standing at the edge of a precipice with no wings, no maps, no first steps. At this moment a teacher, a mentor, a sunrise appeared in my life—Dick Phillips.[39] I see him (and his paintings) as at home with jazz riffs, while conscious of the chord structure and progression. A man studied in all the elements of the visual arts, conducting himself with *unstudied* grace, humor (possible escalation into hilarity) and generosity. I began to trust myself more and more to the process, to the dialogue with the piece itself, risking more of my pigments, more of my paper, more of me.

I've always wanted to be admired for what I do. Though I only admitted that to myself far into my adulthood. I paint to express myself. I paint to get lost in the process. I paint to feel at home. The wanting admiration factor, long in the picture, running at around 90%, has been seen now. It was during a time in my life where I continually felt I had to be *special* to belong. Self-expression, ecstasy (or having time go away) and centeredness were the other 10%. That's pretty much reversed now, and I am grateful.

I still hope some expression of mine, in line and form and color will win a prize, capture a viewer, garner a great price. The more I lean into *these*, the greater the chance I'll freeze, or pace in front of the page, the paper, the canvas. Procrastination. Will it be good enough? It *is* human to measure ourselves. While the canvas is still blank, we all might be Picassos. After it's not, most wonderfully we're all ourselves. A new opportunity to express and experience *all* the nuances of the bouquet, not just Pablo's.

Art, I believe, is not *how* we express ourselves. It is *that* we express ourselves. *All* of us. Our big art is our lives. And for the most part it just comes through. We get to be there when it happens.

And if my painting, my image on a wall, can mirror back to you some truth or beauty you love about yourself, some wonder you have hidden from yourself—what a grace-filled, grace full bonus for us both. And for *me*—what a lucky "job" I have. What a lucky lifetime.

God the Potter

God, Source, Life,
is being "handy" with us
as we and world
turn through our seasons.
We can resist
and go all wobbly.
Or surrender,
welcome the unwelcome—
and return
to center.

Holy Harvey/Whole World

Holy Harvey
Holy deluge
Holy crap
The mighty ocean
Stops its waving
Jumps its gulf
Flies to heaven
Back down as sheet,
Sheet, sheet,
With undercover
Undercurrent.
Lethal blanket
Everywhere.

Waving now
Is just from roofs
And gables,
Boatless, homeless
Once they leave
The premises and promises
Of stability
Of steady home stead
Housing now as
Fleeting as the body
For the soul.

Home is where
The broken heart is
Or lands.
There must be land under there.

There are many hands up here
Up here where
The young carry
Their young
And the old
Carry their dogs
And the strong
Carry the young
And the old.

Seven million two-leggeds
In just this one
Spit of geography
Don't hang up the phone
It's not a lottery
The disconnect moves
You *back* to the *end*
Of the line.

Will we need seven million here?
To be strong?
One for each of us?

Oh yes, for each
A boater, a finder,
A blanket giver
A clothes sorter
A phone worker
Light worker
Traffic general

Food handler
High truck driver
Red Cross worker
Chopper pilot
Raft loader
Weather reader
Cajun Navy captain
Coast guarder
Man in blue
Woman in brown
Flash-aging boy
Quick-thinking girl
Hashtag donor
Facebook poster—

Oh, and all the rest—
Pray-ers,
Dry, warm pray-ers
Sending
Love and Light
And heart
And strength.

And me as one
Wishing now
I *was* a
Cellphoner
To shrink my
Images and their weight
Off my wall
And into
My hand.

Harvey in *my* hand.
Grand illusion.

"He's got the whole world
In Her hands."
Grand solution.

Not timely enough for me,
But...let it be...
Let it be.

Snow

This one is from writers group: "Snow." 20 minutes.

Snow in the desert. It's like the two Irishmen that walked out of a bar...it *could* happen.

The shock of it turned to splendor when Sedona wore its robe for a day.

I was blessed with witnessing Oak Creek Canyon from top to bottom on a return trip after we, Sue and I, found her car in Flagstaff. A friend needed it to go to Flag the night before an early morning hospital procedure. We found I-17 clear. Even with the scarcity of Arizona snow plows. The sun was out but not in eraser mode. The white on either side of us remained. On the pines, the greatest stand of Ponderosa on the planet. Flocks and flocks of them. Flocked and flocked they were.

Return was 89a—I am solo now. Sue is staying to visit her friend. I am ribboning, switch-backing the carving of earth we call Oak Creek Canyon. O.C.C.—Oh see! See!

Everything in its ingredients effulgent with crystalline whiteness. Matching the Sycamore. Contrasting the creek. Giving way finally to Sedona, the lovely lady wearing her once in a century wrap. Bluff after mesa after spire, glowing with presence and pride and wrapping me up in the cold and warm embrace of her newness.

Rudolph

Christmas is over. I love almost everything about it. But "Rudolph," I'm sorry, is the most egregious gang bullying tale/fable I've ever heard. Maybe it's the effect Covid had on the season, leaving me more time and reasons to examine *everything*. And I've loved this song. And my kids have. And the world does.

And yet we have here a grouping in society laughing at, trivializing, name calling, ostracizing by not choosing, one of their "own." Because of a *difference*.

And only with the intervention of a mythical powerful being, saying he's ok, could he be deemed worthy of inclusion. And even *that* is because he was functionally handy, *and* could "save the day." Or "the night," as it were.

And then there's this instantaneous reversal of the tribe's mentality, all the way to *love*. "Then how (they) *loved* him." Why? Because he was one of *them*. *And* he was/would be *famous*. "You'll go down in history." "And *I... knew him*."

"Personal friend."

"*I* was his bff."

Reminding me of a friend, Allah, who was telling my wife and me about a conversation he had with a young nephew, wherein he asked the young teen what he wanted to be when he grew up. To which the young one said, "Famous!" Allah's response: "Famous? *Jack the Ripper* was famous!" And he was able to steer his nephew more into what "lit him up." A *different* approach to a being's inherent light.

So "poor" Rudolph, made "poor" by his peers, who was not looking for fame, or fortune, but just to belong, became a "hit." He went viral with *his* tribe *and* the world. And now the ages. We don't know how hollow or fulfilling this "fame" was for him. It would have to have been in the next verse, had *I* written the song. I *did* write a verse in my book, *Songprints*, that says:

> "I'll sing of what we *share,*
> *and celebrate* the differences."

So I'm sorry Gene. (I always liked Roy better). *And,* bear (or reindeer) in mind, these reflections come from one who has done his share of dealing with "I must be *special* (and *keep* being special) to belong."

I remain however, and as always, a big lover of Christmas and its magic and its myths, and its mysteries.

So, to all you Donners and Blitzens and Rudolphs out there:

> Happy trails to you.
> And to all a good night.

(Santa…has left…the chimney).

The Runner and the Raven

I have a friend.

He is black.

He is a pilot.

He's also the aircraft.

He's making a nest.

We meet early mornings.

Here at Mingus High School's track.

I run. He flies. And lands. And flies.

He hardly ever lands on land here. (Artificial grass?).

He rarely lands lower than the top of the giant light towers, on one of which he is building a home. Right on the platform *humans* use, though rarely, to change or fix the lights.

I have taken to conversing with him. Our usual exchange is three "cru-uks," two syllables, ascending notes, back and forth we go. On the fourth set I respond with "hellos," two syllables, ascending notes. Then I drop out. I'm not sure why I do this. Partly to not interfere with any mate-call this might be. And maybe, since I've read and heard he can imitate sound, to establish I'm from another tribe. And I won't be climbing the stadium light pole with any straw in my beak.

Sometimes, as a couple of other elders from *his* tribe join him and sit and caw on poles and fences and trees surrounding the track, I fantasize they are singing their Marco Polo "where-are-you?" code. In reality it might just be morning conversation. Like, "Great updrafts, eh?" or "Check out old Joe. He's lost a stride or two, hasn't he?"

Most mornings, though, it's just the two of us. *This* morning finds me low. Some family news. And a shrinking pool of jobs I can physically do. With standing all day and/or capacity for lifting up to 50 lbs. with no "accommodation" off the table for me. And the *need I wish I didn't have* for a *job*. After a self-employed lifetime—living from the fruits of my creations and blessed with enough willing participants—up to this 80th year of mine.

He seemed to appear when troubling things and felt needs began arising in me, all coalescing with some urgency. It started with flybys. Close, but not threatening, right over my head, or right in front of my face. I felt blessed by his presence. By his dramatic and solitary exception to his flight plan here. Always at great altitude, save for me.

Then came his first landing on the *fence* that surrounds the track. At eye level for me. Through the years and seasons many small, young ravens have landed and foraged on the ground and track here. Always in flocks. At my approach, in whatever lane—they would disperse. Whoosh away.

He lands on the fence. I am in the lane next to it. I approach. Full stride. He stays. And stays. A couple of laps for me. A long stay for him. I thank him out loud. I was the solo human this day. He the solo great bird. Two souls, athletes. Connecting. I tear. Then stream.

★ ★ ★

I have been running with ravens for years here. None like him. None, of his maturity, who had included me in their flight plan. None who had come any lower than the light tower. Much less eye to eye with me, in his stillness. Just two days ago he entered our "conversation" with a really muted, mournful sounding caw. "Cruuuh." One syllable. Descending. It sounded like mine. It certainly *felt* like mine.

Now here he is. A companion? Sentry? Escort? As I do things only *I* can do. Feeling the loneliness in "*only I*" can do. The things of reconciliation with death, with the next segment of my life or lap en route, with degrees of diminishment and decline, felt loss of usefulness, specialness. Feeling life re-arrange my take on myself at most every level.

In this, the 16th spring season of my running here, even the little ones (following his lead?) when they land in great numbers on the field and fence, don't scutter and scurry and race each other in a quick fly away from me. They let me pass between them. Among them.

As I write this, the season, the nest, my friend and little friends are still here. This morning I ran at a widely variant, earlier time from my usual, and nobody but me showed up.

I needed to see him. Even in the darkness I had begun in. Could he, would he be a guide for me? In whatever I'm involved in here? I ask the Universe for a sign. Even if it's only one *I* would get. As the sun rose on this early spring day, I see a tree in the far distance, beyond the fence, at the end of a row of leafless sisters. A tree with full plumage, its top sticking out above the others. As I run toward it on the long home straightaway, the shape its top forms with its foliage, becomes clearly—a raven. A nested raven. As I hit the turn, and a new view, it morphs into the shape of a beginning-to-*fly* raven. On its way to "on the wing."

I stop in my tracks. I breathe hard. I ask my Spirit brother if there will be a new Spring for *me*, in some new dimension, a new nest, a new sky, a new adventure.

Quothe the Raven: Evermore. Evermore.

Quothe the Runner: Lead on. Lead on.

And help my unbelief.

I start again.

★   ★   ★

Before returning to the earth-bound companion I am blessed to share *this* adventure with. And break fast.

And in the Realm

And in the realm of Truth meets mirth (could we not all use this now?) this, from one of my favorite contemplatives, Sandy Tillotson:

I am who I am, whether I know it or not.

Which reminded me of:

I allow my human nature to unfold in accordance with its destiny,
I remain as I am.
Sri Nisargattada Maharaj.

And this:

When I know from my heart,
It's all *luminous.*
Joe Wise

Pauline and Shipping/ Giving and Receiving

I see her at the track,
Pauline. She works for the school,
For the kids. Mingus High.
She punches in
At shipping and receiving.
Rides her cart
To the outlying lot
And collects the parking fee (wha-at??)
From the elders,
The seniors and juniors
Who have no space
Closer to class.
New this year.
She began blessing them with
"Have a good day."
In the interchange,
A dollar a blessing.

Some now beat her to the punch
With *their* wish for *her*,
Along with their dollar.

A few bringing coffee
They bought on the way.
For her.

Will they learn things
I wonder
As precious
As this
In the building
We call "school?"

Hope so.
I want to trust so.

Accidental Gift? June 1992

Let everything happen to you,
beauty and terror.
Just keep going.
                    Rainer Maria Rilke

We put in at Cotopaxi, got out at Royal Gorge, got back in at Royal Gorge and out near Canyon City. The bus back was quiet for us. Exuberant and loud for everybody else.

What we put in was ourselves. Me, Maleita, my wife, and Michelle, our daughter. What we put ourselves *in* was a yellow rubber raft, and what we put ourselves *into* was the capable hands of a crack rapids runner of international renown *and* the froth and force of the Arkansas River, swollen considerably by recent winter melt and runoffs.

Maleita and I had come out West from Kentucky, visiting Michelle for a couple of her free days in Denver, and would be going on to other as yet to be determined spots, locations, in Colorado and/or New Mexico. It is the 90s and pre-everything's-on-your-phone America, or on-your-phone world for that matter.

So, I believe I picked up the brochure at maybe a Denny's, after breakfast, from a rack on the way out. *Whitewater rafting at its finest. See Royal Gorge, if you dare. It may demand so much attention you don't even notice the Royal Gorge Bridge 1053 feet above the river.* That sounded too dangerous. Surely they'll have "bunny" runs as well. Or at least "intermediate" ones.

I'd never been whitewater rafting. Sort of a bucket list item for me. I wasn't interested however in having it be the *last* on my list, by dint of *kicking* it. Maleita and Michelle thought it would be fun, *and* thrilling, and so we headed to Nathrop, home base of our tour guides, an hour or so down the road.

We begin by suiting up. And I get a light tickling of heat, fear. All over. Elaborate and voluminous outer wear. I had figured a life vest would be about it. We begin by squeezing into a full body wet suit. And squeezing had very little to do with body weight or shape. It was designed to be *skin tight*. It took a surprising amount of strength to pull it on. Some of my maleness, macho-ness was beginning to leak into my persona. *I'm not cancelling because I can't get this on.* Wrestling. It happens. Both the leak, *and* success with the vestiture. We could keep our shoes, but the large tech-laden vests and NFL-looking helmets were mandatory. *This is a lot of protection.* For what basically is a river ride. It had not fully entered my mind how crucial *rocks* were to the course, to the side bounds, to the faceting of flows, to the spray and bounce, to the solid step downs, and the craggy ones. *Oh-kaay.*

We all, other bucket-listers I guess, gather in a larger room, to await directions. One of the outfitters who oversaw our family's gearing up, came up to us and said, "You can go on the six-seater raft down one of the courses on one of the trips you asked about, *or* you can go on a four-seater with one of the best in the world on the half day Royal Gorge one. *He's just* become available." This trip is the one their own brochure describes as having huge waves, steep "technical drops" and almost "continuous whitewater rapids." Among these are ones named Sledgehammer, Wallslammer, the Narrows, Boateater, and the "infamous" Sunshine Falls. *They do this every day,* I tell myself as I turn to Michelle and Maleita for a decide huddle. I am about 40% wanting *this* one, and 100% not wanting to look anything but brave.

We want the best they have on the scariest run. I doubt any one of us formulated it that way in the moment, but we locked in on the Royal Gorge. The safety factor (to some unknown power) that was added in here: our rafter/captain would handle both oars. We were free to just enjoy, flinch, tolerate, or be terrorized by the ride. Maybe all four. All that was required of *us* was to "be in good physical condition." We were.

The room empties out and the bus fills up. Heading to Cotopaxi for our "put in," port. Lots of jabber and, I suspect, conjured hale and hearty bravado, blows up the balloon of all our excitement and trepidation. I become aware of a serious-minded, leather-skinned thirty-something holding forth in the aisle. The only hint of *gravitas* on the vehicle. I move closer.

He's a safety instructor. About rafts. And the rivers they ride in. And things that can happen. His sun-seasoned skin and *really good* physical condition help me believe he knows whereof he speaks. Mostly, I suspect, from his *own* captain's logs.

I feel drawn to listen as if we were the only two in this crowded mobile room. In my teens I was trained and certified by the Red Cross as a lifeguard. In my twenties trained and certified as a water safety instructor. Not much of that related to what he was saying. No pool, pond, lake or ocean scenes. Only the rocks and the rapids-rich Arkansas. I listen and lock it all in.

Off the bus. *Our* guide is friendly, fit, *and professional*, i.e. *appropriately* friendly. No discussions of his latest divorce or things he has done with a Harley. He is assured in his launching sequence and keeps apprising us of things we may not have picked up on. My butterflies are on board. They've picked up on about everything since I opened the brochure. Larry, his name, moves gracefully. In the plus column. He places me toward the front, with him. Maleita and Michelle balance each other in the back. The raft is almost a square compared to the six-seater plump rectangles. We're off.

It looks like there's a small flotilla involved. Bright yellow rubber rafts. I wonder how many are going all the way, i.e. to the Gorge. None of the captain/guides look nervous. *Plus column.*

The day is overcast and a bit chilly, but the ride pays no mind and delivers a knockout opening jitterbugging slalom sequence. Whew! Catch a breath, glide, wooah? Slam, by water, not rock, *plus column* lean, lift up, hold on…Bam! Belly wop (yellow belly takes the blow)…*plus,* twist hard, can't see through the spray, shift quick and fly again, slick landing and…exhale. A break. Moving pretty fast, but a peril (hazard?) break.

First time we three lock eyes. All brows are up. Hesitant smiles. Not an ounce of validity in any of them. Larry looks cool. The rest of us do too, in a different way. Spray wet cool. Great idea, the wetsuits. *Plus.*

The next segment, as wild as it was, was beginning to feel, God help me, routine. And no doubt we were flying by and into and around all the ones (Wallslammer? Boateater?... those) with names. The ones I told myself I'd really take note of. These have got to be viewable and identified only from the shores, where they're a location. Out here, they're an experience. I started to say "only" an experience. There is no "only" in any part of this ballistic, yellow projectile fat-barreled cannon shot.

We've now entered our longest and widest water glide yet. I look ahead on this relative "table" of water, see an infinity pool ending and start to wonder if this would have been the most feared thing in a telescope on the Nina, the Pina, or the Santa Maria a few hundred years ago. This had to be the #6 the Bus Man spoke of. Boaters and rafters, it turns out, have a fairly universal numbered scale for the severity of the challenge in a stream event. They top out at 6 (or 7 in some scales) as the most, well, dangerous. The Bus Man ominously (to me) called it a "hole."

Our raft picks up speed. Larry straightens and takes a deep breath. His eyes, lasers. He grips and re-grips his oars. I find myself watching *only* him and escalating toward my highest level of physical fear. All generated at times when I was completely removed from control. Mostly in aircrafts of various constructions. Larry's face starts to look like a big league hitter facing a hundred mile an hour pitch of a really *hard* ball. You have to stand in the batter's box to be able to hit it. Or have it hit *you.* We are right at the edge of the ledge. Another raft is passing us (this hasn't happened before). Larry's focus is not on the passer. They knock the left oar out of his hand and out of our raft as we plunge, plunge into the hole…

We're miraculously upright...I look to Larry...maybe not so miraculous. He's flailing with one oar to move us out of this new kind of turbulence. We are circling ourselves...the face of futility frustration, fear, all Larry's, is the last thing I see before I am thrown.

This is where the clock starts, and the clock stops. The clock starts on my time underwater. The clock stops on *everything else.* Starting in 8th grade I would practice holding my breath. In my teens and twenties even more. I was scuba diving by then. Between 2 and 3 minutes I could count on. No recent practice, but I've been a distance runner since I was 12. All this is negated, taken away, by the temperature of and rapid immersion in the water. Lesson one from the bus man: *Should you go overboard, your body will reactively and immediately expel any air you have.* Breath gone. Check.

I am a *strong* swimmer. And a *distance* swimmer. Once about 3 miles in the Ohio (River). Lesson number two: *If you go in the hole, it will hold you, till it doesn't. This will be before or after you drown.* **I WILL** be the exception. I'll *bust* out. No check yet.

I can't find up. Lesson number three: *While in the hole the life vest will be ineffective.* Check. I make motions to swim in any one direction. Futile. No movement. The only movement is the incessant, rampaging movement of water, holding me inside a sideways(?) vertical(?) whirlpool or churn. I became extremely aware I'm close to reflexively having to fill my lungs with the only thing available. And that I can (and do) put a check by number two. *Physically*, it's up to the water and its turbulence right here. I picture myself (I still have no cues to activate proprioperception) "standing" in the relatively calm center of this whirling water wall. I am surrendering to what's next.

As I write this, it is curious that my arms were up, bent at the elbows, a classic surrender pose. My legs were similarly bent at the knees, a classic pre-swimming out pose. "Readiness" for either?

No real psychological readiness for anything other than **more life**. Churn...churn. **Earth life**! Churn, churn...**I want to live**! Churn, churn...I had survived alcohol and depression and an incredible (to me) life change...churn, churn... ...**Whoosh. Pop!** I break surface. I am thrown out of the hole...oh my God...oh my God... **Rocks!**

I'm in with the rocks now. *I* am the raft. *I* take the blows. Bus man in my ear, *Get on your back.* Check. *Point your feet downstream.* Check. *Angle yourself slightly toward the closest shore.* Check. *Paddle backwards with your arms.* Check. *Let your feet hit the rocks…Push off—continue shoreward.* Check. Oh happy alive check! Push off. Paddle. Push off. Paddle… A kayaker appears over my shore shoulder. She's in fairly calm water. I'm close to "her" eddy. Through the water's roar I hear, "Grab on!" I reach the tip of her hull. We make shore.

I stand immediately, wobbly inside my body, wobbly on rocks, and yell across the wide river, to people, several people, dry and wet, I shout, "MY WIFE?" "MY WIFE!"

"She's over here! She's ok!"

I don't get my next shout from my heart to my lips ("Where's my daughter?") before I see her, being helped, making her way toward me, on "my" shore. One shoe. Some blood. *All* there. All here. "We're" all here.

Apparently no other rafts, nobody else, went in. I later hear our whole raft, including the raft itself, went under, was *pulled* under.[40] I was just the first one in.

Scattered picture and word fragments from this point are all that get in and remain. Larry's face, chastened, shoulders slumped, dead eyes. "We can't get out here…No way out of the canyon… Back in the raft." Forever on the river. Cold. Freezing cold. Body questioning…*in the water, not cold. Out, freezing?* Numb. All of me. Bus ride, loud, laughing, continuous. We four, no words. Blank stares. Change-back room. Dry. Re-dress. Standing. Not moving.

Breaking out of my "trance" with a loud laughing voice from behind, in my ear, "I hear you had a lot of adventure out there? Fun, huh?" The manager. I snap. I speak. Loudly. Forcefully. Way beyond my usual "range." Not letting him "invade us," re-write our experience, or trivialize our emotional state. He backs off.

We get in our van and I drive away, with only one intention: find a place to pull over and get out and just be as much me as wanted to surface. It took the form of the three of us standing in triangle/ circle, arms around. Most of the rest for me was release in tears. An "almost lost..." cry on the surface. More release and what is triggered would come later.

Back in the van. Back to Denver. A stop in Colorado Springs. Along with everything else, my borderline hypoglycemia, was making me shaky. This I could attend to immediately, and remedially. Food. It's late now. We find a restaurant still open a bit longer. We have a waitress with a motherly aura who stopped mid-order and asked, "Are you all ok?" Something I like to believe I would have done. In one glance. One heartbeat. Then she blew by all that and sat down to listen to us, hesitantly...debrief ourselves, release some feelings, take new steps out of shock.

The soup was good. She was grace. (Literally, before our meal).

Back at Michelle's apartment. Wordless. Purposeless actions. Nobody untouched enough by trauma to be of comfort. Or un-numb enough to receive it. I recall a moment when I felt the warmth and mercy of exhaustion making its first inroads into the frozen fear-field that was everything else. Sleep. Broken, but sleep. Maleita getting up during the night, having hours earlier seen only her daughter's shoe tossing, bouncing, bobbing downstream on the raging rapids, going back, she tells me, to Michelle's room to see if, to make sure, she is breathing.

Waking at some pre-dawn hour and deciding whether to continue on with our vacation, or go back home, to Kentucky. Thinking we would feel the same in either place, we decide on someplace we could find, close to here, not far, and a place saturated with, *brimming* with...extreme uneventfulness. Who could ever believe its name would be Purgatory?

★ ★ ★

Purgatory in June *is* uneventful. A ski resort complex. Looking like a ghost town. Yeah. We had come up with Durango, because the name was so "Western," but we didn't want to stay in a town. By name, in the vicinity, we lighted on "Woodlands-something," but *it* turned out to be *too* rustic. It's getting late in the day. The only other place near is Purgatory. No. No way. I am not staying in a place called Purgatory. Not today. Not ever. Let's go look.

Wow. Beautiful. Let's stay for eternity. We get a mammoth modern suite loaded with appliances and conveniences and with, well *rooms*, for about 1/10th of the ski season rate. I am close to humming, "Almost heaven, Purgatory..." in honor of the Rocky Mountain High Guy,[41] though *this* one was written by the Danoffs of West Virginia. We both experience a dramatic lift here.

As soon as we got in the room, I changed into my swim trunks and told Maleita I was heading for the (heated) pool. I knew I needed to get right back on the bronco, the bull that threw me. My first act of forgiving the water, and acknowledging *I* knew, in the course it ran, it was a snake. I knew it when I picked it up. Actually when I picked the brochure up. The pool is empty of people. The *week* is, gratefully, pretty much the same, for this mini-village of a resort. I dive deliberately in. Calm water. Warm water.

We also had key access to a hot tub/Jacuzzi spa on the resort's roof. It became a nocturnal, private (no one else came) ritual for us. Go up to the roof, enter the water, lean our heads back on the side, look into the primordial dark, and see how the stars spilled out of God's hand tonight.

★　★　★

The first morning in Purgatory (*there's* a great line I never saw coming), the first morning there, we struck out on a rural walk/hike. Spring in high country Colorado. "Morning has broken..."[42] was my inner soundtrack. There were "first birds" and "first flowers." Even wild grasses and weeds appeared as precious extravagances. I usually run. Today I walk. With Maleita. We hold hands all the way. "I don't want to miss a thing."[43]

★　★　★

Accidental gift. Yes and yes. Yes it was an accident. Not "I fell out of a boat." A *traumatic* accident. I had someone in my extended family ask me at a wedding reception back home, "Did you die? Or your wife or daughter?"

"No," I said, wondering where this was going.

"Then you had a *good* day."

He was uncomfortable. I was defensive. We were, of course, both telling the truth.

An accident, life-threatening. Yet not life-reviewing, for me, as so many seem to experience. Perhaps because I still had *some* hope of getting out of this alive. My focus was on readiness. Personal readiness. To do my part to live. Neither Maleita nor Michelle appeared in my consciousness till I touched shore.

Accidental *gift*. Yes, there have been some. Most, some time after the event. The big early ones were a period of deeply felt gratitude for life. Mine. Maleita's. Michelle's. We had been dear to each other for some time. Dear from birth. *Deer* for several years. After Michelle moved fully into her own life in Colorado, we began to notice every time we were able to gather, calendar and geography wise, there would inevitably be a sighting of three deer by all of us. Several times in several states. Until the last sighting at Grand Canyon. Our last day together there. A shuttle bus was bringing us back from Yaki Point in a drizzle at dusk, and one of us remarked, "Well, this breaks the string I guess." Whereupon the bus driver hit the brakes and announced, "Up here on the left, if you look carefully, you'll see two deer," a brief pause, "and over on the right another deer." He was waiting to see if they would get together. They didn't. Michelle was newly engaged and would marry. This did indeed break the string. Not a string of enmeshment. We had all been strong independent souls. The deer string. D-e-e-r. Not the d-e-a-r one.

Accidental *gift*. I was coming out of a deep depression, mostly related to an unwelcome backlash and emerging fear-based narrowness in the arena I was flourishing in. I felt myself, found myself, saw myself wanting to live, to go on. Even with no clear path. Even if I completely surrendered that work, that career. Not a method for attaining clarity I'd recommend, but it was mine. Unmistakably mine. The words to one of the last songs I had written sprang to consciousness in this aftermath. "Through the raging waters you shall not be drowned. No one takes your life from you, you may lay it down."[44]

Was it also a gift to be assured of in some way I/we would be allowed complicity with the circumstances of our transition, our death? That book is still open. *And* I am still free to work with the greatest *gift* part of all of this. It too is a question. How much energy do I want to give to trying not to lose things? My worry self, my anxious self spends so much of me guarding, or protecting my *things*. My physical things, my rituals, my thoughts, my predictables, my favorite everything. On guard, subtly. Re-minding myself, literally, to not be owned.

And not lose the pearl of great price in the vigil and the vigilance: Me. Divine, whole and complete. As I was created. "Vaster than sky, greater than space."[45] Closer than breathing. I shall not be drowned.

Satsang at Safeway

A Brief Encounter

Her shirt was black and white
And the print was big.
All *words*, too many to get
Without *stalking* the wearer.

Too curious to let it go
I just *asked* her
If I could read her Tee.

She opened her arms.
It was a letter:
Dear Karma,
I have a *list*
Of people you've missed.
Love,
Me.

We were in the ice cream aisle,
Which is how I've worked out
A *lot* of *my* karma.

To a Tee

Man does not live by tee shirts alone. A woman doesn't either. But we sure have a lot of them. And a whole lot of them say something. Something besides "Nike" or "Under Armour." Like it or no, many of us walk around as mobile sandwich boards. Some of us are conscious of the humble garment's megaphonic effect, and make our purchases with its propogating properties in mind. Most with pre-programed bon mots or aphorisms. All likely pre-screened. That is, silk screened, not censored.

And whatever censoring or polite societal maxims we used to employ or operate from seem M. I. A. bigtime. For the most part I find that attractive, liberating, and indicative of a certain overall maturity. In some cases, however, I find myself checking for weapons and/or exits.

Happily, almost all fall between the extremes. Humor has not gone completely AWOL. And in some cases I even find words to live by. Though in general being taught by a tee shirt is pretty much as palatable as unsolicited advice. My happiest, beneficent exception recently was proclaimed, T-claimed by a man at my local gym, "Be present, not perfect." A nice goal, and it reminded me of one of my all-time favorite jokes.

"Past, Present, and Future walked into a bar.

It was tense."

The scariest Tee's I encounter are usually at Walmart. I *do* live in a small town in a way out West western state. I try to factor that in.

One recent encounter with a woman in the automotive aisle shook me. Her Tee read: "Evil keeps me pretty." Besides my immediate assumption our markers for pulchritude were widely divergent, I noticed she was lingering near the antifreeze. And I had just seen yet another Dateline where the tasteless–except–for–sweet properties of ethylene glycol were employed to effect a permanent lawyer-less divorce from a no longer desirable partner. I wondered if that was her mate I could see in the adjoining sports aisle, picking out a new Titanium Driver for his golf set. Or maybe for her head. I've got to watch more Oprah.

One just as scary, but for some reason I chose to make it funny, also announced itself in Walmart. It said, "Dangerously Undermedicated." It helped that he wasn't in the hunting aisle. He was in supplements. Lookin' to get high on Ginkgo biloba? Forget it all with Prevagen? Oh yeah, that's for *memory*. And it's still not available in stores? I forget.

Walmart is not however a complete self-help wasteland, shirt wise, and elders are not the only bearers of torso mirth and good news. On the same day, I saw a toddler with "I didn't do it." And maybe an uncle across the store with "The rum made me do it." Who was a cousin to, "This beer tastes like I'm off tomorrow." I know I saw a dueling mentor pair of men with a child, one man present only on the T-shirt in word. The Tee the gray hair wore said it clearly: "Dad's know a lot. Grandpas know everything."

My all-time favorite though at *this* venue, is courtesy of an energetic youngster yanking away on Mom's hand, shirt proclaiming, "I can play all day." I know he could. His Mom looked like she knew it. And now that I'm *not* raising a kid, I'm thinking of making that *my* life's goal. T get in *that* kind of groove and wear *that* shirt all day. Basically as a disclaimer to any left brain onlookers, especially any licensed or commissioned officers. Like that.

I *did* marvel, at the sophistication and au current-ness of *this* Walmart a few years back, when it began *selling* a tee shirt I chose not to interpret in a *Deliverance* kind of way. It's message: "What happens in Cottonwood... (all together now) stays in Cottonwood."

I'm generally more satisfied and inspired by the tees at the gym. Except for the large strain of them that deal with, well, strain. And I suppose macho-ness. The ones that really help your self-critic along. You know, when he's having a lethargic spell. Like: "Run more than your mouth"—with a big swoosh from the "Just-do-it" people. Perhaps not a blatant all out "shut-up" directive, but a call for more balance. Perhaps wisely a propos for everybody here today. But me.

And then there's the one nobody can escape, except its wearer, "My warm-up is your workout." It wouldn't crank my shame meter so much if it wasn't on a guy who looks 90 in his second hour of aerobic weight work. O Kaaay...

I *do* find some relief in the tees most *women* wear here. They're softer, more human generally. And, in some cases, genuinely inspiring. Last week, in the weight machine area, a new-to-me woman, short and stout and some degrees off American TV /Movie /Magazine beauty standards, wore a large print cotton "voice" that announced, "Woman. Strong. Fearless. Proud." It's on all of us that she needs to be so bold. And it's honorably on her that she is. I won't quibble here about the "fearless," fear I believe pretty much coming as standard equipment in the package we call "human." In general, I take "fearless" as shorthand for "feel the fear and do it anyway."

I guess I've been a word guy as long as I can remember. They've always meant something to me. No throwaways. They are some of our best pointers to Truth. So I find myself drawn to people *who* and things *that* set out to say a lot with a little. Small canvases, like T-Shirts, bumper stickers, book titles, signs. Equal learner, I am.

When I was in the waiting room of my new dentist out here in Arizona, there was a small book on a side table titled, *Don't Squat with Your Spurs on*. I took that as a Western wisdom and not a reference point for the pain level I would soon encounter. Other book titles can become helpful mantras for me. Currently that is Matt Kahn's, *Whatever Arises, Love That*. Or its corollary, Mary O'Malley's, *What's in the Way, Is the Way*. I also found out you can't copyright a title. So I can feel free to use it here or anywhere. In fact, I was gonna call *this* book *Gone With the Wind*, but at 78, it might be an unwelcome self-prophecy. I'm sticking with "Volume III" of...something.

Bumper stickers come and go, and of course that's part of their charm, and their purpose, the DNA of their destiny. I have two faves that both go for the cosmic level. Number one, "I don't know. And you don't either." Number two, but no lesser an offering, "What if the Hokey Pokey *is* what it's all about?" Then there's the bumper sticker I saw not on a bumper, but on the rear of the body of the car itself. It was a Smart car. The sticker said, "Actual size."

Sometimes a short-lived visual accompanied by a pithy, that is to say brief (and not what a speech aberration might alter it to sound like)...that is to say, a pithy comment with a spontaneous visual can rise to the level of a good tee or title or b'sticker. On a recent trip to Basha's supermarket in Sedona, I am waiting in line with my two apples, Romaine lettuce and several protein bars already on the currently still belt, awaiting the man-in-front-of-me's transactions to be complete, and a gentleman comes in behind me and deposits *his* items on the belt. A container of Tillamook extra creamy vanilla bean ice cream and a pint of Bulleit brand whiskey. He looks at me: "Breakfast of champions."

And I'll close with *my* champion. Champions, really. Two. Two tees. Neither a mulligan. Both keepers. The first, coming out of the library. Libraries, the locus of the vastest reservoir of human history, thought, wisdom and information anywhere, with the exception of what creates that flat bulge in your pocket and unchecked, announces itself at the deepest moments of the community's silent meditation. This one's wearer and bearer, an elderly woman, face and body long in the fray. Just three words. "C'est la vie." I translate as "It's allowed." "Let it be." A fine mantra. Reminding me to ask myself if I want to live in constant resistance to Reality. Noticing when I do surrender or acquiesce it's not so much because of spiritual discipline, but for the relief of it, embracing *me and* the world just as we are at this moment. *Change*, which inevitably turns out to be *mine*, in some form or fashion, then becomes an option.

The second, the grand finale tee walks into the room on a 30ish man with a 30ish woman, a room where I am already expectant of relaxed sacraments, signs concerning the core of things. Out-picturings of all the beauty in ordinary things. It is my favorite (as it is for many) local mom and pop eatery, Pepe's. If I am not greeted by St. Peter as I am by Pepe, I may want to go back. The core of things. Gathering. Welcoming. Attending to. Feel-at-homeness. *Cheers* without a bar. Good food, fresh ingredients, reasonable prices, friendly staff.

I don't get to read all of his shirt before he sits in the booth next to me. The tee message itself, as much as I had read of it, was enough to embolden me, as I was just leaving, to stop and "get" the rest. It said: "Untied Dyslexics Church of Dog." My Church. I'm there. I'm going. But I'm there. Church of Dog. That's ok *nine* days out of nine. Ten out of ten. *And*, no dog*ma*, unless it's a Bitchop.

Yep, suits me to a Tee.

$$\star \quad \star \quad \star$$

There was this one find that *could* have ended my small canvas quest. In an eclectic shop with cards, soaps, signs, earrings, scarves and such, there was a small offering on a window that read: "If you're looking for a sign, this is it."

What's in a Word?

As I was selecting and proof reading pieces for this collection I was struck with how much this particular writing reflects my "finding my way." Words and self-talk became important in a new way to me in my 40s when in the midst of all my strivings I became aware I might "think" of myself as a husband, not the husband, a father, not the...an artist... The relief of even beginning to think of myself this way felt so true and liberating and peaceful, I began to live a more examined word, and heretofore mostly "hidden," self-talk life. Not that I sit with this often, but I'm more aware of its significance to me and would like to see how it might impact the world as we all live our lives on the fly. This piece reflects my journey with this process so far. Including the seriousness of the inquiry, and the easy, perspective-keeping side tracks of word-humor that pop up. I remind myself it is a piece about this process... and a journey, not a destination or arrival.

All words imprison what they name. Some are more distorting than others. And often not obviously. Some spiritual self-masters teach that naming anything or anyone can be the beginning of lessening or de-valuing. Words take on their truest, most beneficent properties, when we see and know them as pointers. Not as the *real* thing. No matter how many times I *say* the word "water," it will never be wet. Of course for shorthand and discourse, words are stars.

And when we view words as *expressions*, as the Master from Galilee taught, *he* and *we* are the Words of the Divine Source—Expressions, or literally the "squeezed outness" of the Christ consciousness, what God looks like as me.

The "harmful words," words that don't serve at the least, and help create distance, judicial stances, and outright rejection at the most,[46] are more and more, I believe, being seen for the fear bullets or bombs they are. Weapons we pull out when we're afraid we don't know the true landscape—it may be shifting, we feel threatened in status, belonging, or possessions. In short, when our judge is in session,[47] often without consciously noticing it, and assume ourselves the only arbiter and supreme court of reality.

The easiest one of these to identify is "should" and cousins "ought," "must," and "have to." Who's in charge here? Who says what here? And as a fine little folk song by David Roth says, "Don't *should* on me and I won't *should* on you."[48] I think that phrase "should" be... (oops) *I'd like to see* that phrase added in to the wedding vows. And while we're at the wedding, let's talk about "vows" and "promises." I'm sometimes uncomfortable with either. "Promise" has too many variables, including some you won't see or can't see coming, and won't have any control over. How about "intend." 'I intend to die with you..." Well, that's not working out so well either. But "I intend" or "I set my intention to honor you, to be willing to be with you in poverty or wealth—or the non-existent middle class. I intend to hang with you when things are going well and you are well, and well that's all I got for now."

The added benefit here is, a realistic scenario for not having to make ourselves feel like a serial "failure," at the outset of a new kind of together-life, like any life, a life of re-calibration and re-intending. And Yoda won't let us get by with "try." "*Do* or not *do*." "Make an effort" after "setting our intention," seems reasonable and "do"-able.

There are a couple of words I find subtle and almost innocent at first blush. "Worthy" and "deserve." What I've come to know is once you admit/posit "worthy," you're setting up "not worthy" at the same level, in the same house. Who's the judge here? In sports, or chess, or games, it's satisfying to have a "worthy" opponent—one who can bring out the best in both of us. But what of the eleventh hour worker,[49] in the famous parable, being paid the same as the all-day laborers? The story only comes alive when we question the "deserve" factor, and who gets to decide.

With "right" and "wrong" and "good" and bad," I relate to the wisdom and poetry of the Bard, William Shakespeare—"There is nothing either good or bad, but thinking makes it so."[50] Most of the time "good" for me means *I* feel more comfortable and pleased. Of course societal mores are valuable for safety and harmonious growth, but I find a lot of my/our pronouncements with "good" or "bad" to be subtly divisive and stratifying.[51]

"Positive" and "negative" are pretty much shipmates with "good" and "bad." Crucial in electronics, math and magnetic fields, they don't seem very useful with say—emotions. Linking "bad" with "negative," and labeling anger or fear as "bad" for instance, feels like at least a slap at evolution, if not a critique of the Creator's design. Here again for me "positive" often means I like it. "Negative," I don't.

I'll close with a few of, at least for me, most soul-stymying, edict-bearing subtle judge-words that masquerade as truth in a most hidden way. "Stuck" is such a one. It's one, that used or thought only re-enforces a falsehood/judgement and prolongs, righteously, the resulting condition. When I am lucky enough to catch that one on board my thought train, I like to leave him off at the next station and pick up his more truthful cousin, "I'm here in a place for longer than I am comfortable." And there is always choice. "Always" being a rarely used spice, along with its counterpart "never," as everything changes. This too shall pass—"good," "bad" or indifferent. To be honest with you, "indifferent" is my favorite of the three. The least judgmental, the most peaceful.

"To be honest with you" is more than one word, but it often appears as "frankly," "honestly," even "candidly" and makes me wonder about all the things that came before or will come after. What was that? What will that be?

And finally, there is "finally." As in, I finally learned to ski. Or I finally graduated. Who's keeping the clock here? Where did that enter my field? Who's voice? Are they in my corner? Am I in my own corner?

Not sure how to end this. I'm stuck. I'm uncomfortable. Frankly, I'm through. Finally through. Oh well, *One outa' four ain't bad.*[52]

Two for the Show/Earth Life

There are two "definitions" of enlightenment I resonate with.

The first is Pema Chödrön's (the principal teacher at Gampo Abbey in Nova Scotia): "Relaxing into life."

The second is anonymous: "We give up
                         what we made up
                         to wake up."

★　★　★

We are born it seems with blinders. Like those of a skittish race horse. Readied for our "Run for the Roses." In the human race.

We have added on other handicaps. By others. By ourselves.

There is the imprint of the first six years. (And any teen or adult trauma.)

And the rest of our lives processing it.

Learning to live with it.

Not die from it.

Sometimes slowly. Sometimes quickly.

Becoming aware. Acknowledging. Welcoming. Listening. Learning from. Moving on, till (or if) "it" appears again.

Honoring our courage.

Remembering who we really are. Newly aware it is not *these things,* that we thought defined us.

And if we are super lucky, we have parents and elders that oversee our childhood, who *see us* for who we are, help minimize the blinders and the misinformation, and stand with us in our strength and in our weakness, encourage us, guide us toward our own course, as we find our unique place in the human field, the human race. Ok with whoever wins the roses, knowing we all share the garland. We are all blooming. Blinders and all.

Jemez Springs

Up on Sunday.
In New Mexico.
Morning drive out.
Let the road take us.

It took us alone, like astronauts in outer space, to the open hills, with timeless cattle grazing far and near. It took us to the waking mountains, brightening, coloring with the sun. It took us to the wild flowers, staging beauty sprays and gay Terpsichore at every turn. And then a town. Small. Quaint? *Old*, it seemed. We are on vacation, Maleita, my wife, my travel buddy and I. Second one in the West. We're on a blue road, two steps down from Interstate. Two laner in the country. No megalopolis in sight. Just right.

The small sign declares "Jemez Springs" is this settlement. No traffic. No lights or stop signs. The *large* sign, biggest in the two block "heart" of town, above the porch of a saloon-like structure proclaims, "*World's Best Pancakes.*" We smile and roll by. Still no *people* in sight. Maybe still at church. Haven't seen one of *those* in town either. New Mexico is riddled with churches on blue roads, maybe as densely as any state in the union. Maybe Jemez Springs doesn't need one.

We hadn't planned on finding a Sunday service. Our spiritual "home" was already in flux, even in a got one-of-every-kind metropolis back in Kentucky. Quaker and Unity communities and services seemed the most satisfying so far. But we were yet to explore anything from the Eastern Hemisph...bam! Up jumps a Buddhist monastery. With a big welcome sign for non-monks today. The car turned itself in. We found and joined a sitting silent meditation group in a spare, wood-rich room. Some monks. A few non. The silence was rich. Pregnant. Expectant. *And* relaxed. I contribute. I receive.

The day's facilitator, in monastery garb, eased us out of the silence, then asked us to *maintain it* as we moved outside to the courtyard and garden area, where he instructed and led us, literally, in walking meditation. Meditation on the move, so to speak. All of us walking slowly in file, eyes down, conscious of our step, the rhythm, our breathing, and the day (which was a *beaut*).

When he stopped, and we became rail cars, one by one snugging up to our predecessor, all coming to complete rest, he invited us back indoors to a large sunroom, running almost the width of the monastery. Furnished with what you'd expect, and occupied currently only by several baskets of what looked like short, long-dead, twigs, still clinging to their leafage. These are, it turns out, dried herbs or spices, from the monks' garden. Our next experience will be, sitting on the floor, again in silence, removing each dried leaf, blossom, kernel or bloom from its stem, one at a time, and placing them in an adjoining basket, while depositing the then bare twig onto its own neighboring thatch-pile.

I find myself eyeing everyone else's basket to see if distribution has been equitable. I'm guessing this is not a good "mindfulness" start. I set about my task. In the quiet. The quiet being in the room. In *me*, not so much. I am only on my second twig when the industrial revolution takes over my weak mind, and begins to pepper it (excuse the pun) with all kinds of efficiency critiques *and* world changing innovations. Like holding the twig at the end with one hand and putting the other hand next to it in a pinch and letting that one travel rapidly down the line right over the repository, the grateful hungry basket. *This* is why communal silence is hard. I *could* just stand up and mime this. Heck I could demonstrate it outright.

Nobody else looks like they're in tune with this mind stream. They are not looking around. They are not hurrying. Is there no such thing as a fast monk? I had heard lunch was next, and the piles needed to rise. They did. Their pace, glacial.

When lunch time *was* announced, and we were invited, it was described to us as, being in silence, and consisting of all, and only, raw and organic vegetables of many exotic stripes. Maleita and I eyed each other, and I spoke for us both with, "What a generous and delightful offering, but I'm afraid we have another appointment we must see to."

A bow and thanks. Out to the car. Seated. Breaking our silence together, "World's Best...?" You bet.

I was going to sit close enough to the kitchen to smell the buttermilk infused batter and relish the sound and sizzle of thick dense Canadian bacon, all the while feeling over and over the sticky on the maple syrup cruet. And when my stack arrived, head off all incoming thought trains about industrial innovations, take up my old fashioned fork and become *extremely* mindful during each languid round trip it took from my plate to me.

I am happy to report how successful I was.

★ ★ ★

Pancakes. The "greatest" made even "greater" by how much attention I paid to them. Not unlike the awakening process, to my Self. The divine essence of (my) Self.

Mindfulness. Do what you are doing. This is way too easy to be discovered. And almost anathema in a social media world. Even one like mine, with no twitter, texting, snapchat, facebook, or *cellphone*.[53] There's enough in my everyday life to wonder what I'm missing, while I'm missing what I'm currently *doing*.[54] Writing for me, seems to be an exception. And great gift. That, and someone else's presence. When I commit to either I don't feel deprived. Or like I'm missing anything. More like peace and engagement.

I set my intention to daily expand the activities and non-activities that generate this result. Are we designed this way? Do what you do, to be who you be? In the case of silent sitting, is the goal to be like the two monks deep in meditation, and the one leans over to the other and says, "Are you not thinking of what I'm not thinking of?" I lean toward "yes" just because it makes me smile. "Effortless efforting," Adya calls it. Adyashanti, a Western/Eastern long-time unknowing teacher of mine, mostly from afar, books, cds, podcasts, you tubes. Some near. When he comes to Sedona. He who calls himself a "failed meditator."

And when it comes to doing what I'm doing with more and more efficiency and speed, I recall the tale of the young seeker coming to the Buddhist monastery and being welcomed by the Zen master with a tea ceremony of some elaboration and duration. At the end of which the neophyte says, "Master, I can make all of this go so much faster with this new invention called the microwave. We could have tea in two minutes." There was a considerable considered silence before the elder replied, "Why would I *want* to do *that*?"

And in its recall, this tale, I'm always hoping it helps take me back to Jemez Springs, and an invitation to "choose again," whenever I find myself speed- stripping the herbs and spices in my flash-forward life, in Cottonwood.

★   ★   ★

What is a pace I can do with the most peace for me, without having "the world" run over me? How much news to watch? How much cave dwelling? How much activity surfing? A balance to be sought, along with and as, the pearl of great price.[55]

Song of the Wounded, (Love is Gentle)

Lyrics

Refrain
Love is gentle, love is kind,
Gives the room and takes the time,
Plays the softest melody,
Till you find your harmony.
Love is gentle, love is kind,
Walks around inside your mind,
Opens doors and leaves the key,
Finds the why of you and me.

Take it slow with me,
Just let me grow and be free,
And I'll shoot a thousand tendrils up
To touch your morning sky.
Take your sweet time with me,
Come make a rhyme with me,
Watch me flow, and let me wash you when I cry.

Refrain

Instrumental

Don't be so sure of me,
Don't make a cure of me,
Bless my wings,
Then let me find my piece of sky.

Refrain
Love is gentle, love is kind,
Gives the room and takes the time,
Plays the softest melody,
Till you find your harmony.
Love is gentle, love is kind,
Walks around inside your mind,
Opens doors and leaves the key,
Finds the why of you and me...

Waltz me around and hear the sound you know I've got to give.

Noah

Song of the Wounded/Love is Gentle
Song Stories

"The wounded" he called them.

And he had seen "the wounded" in the survivors of the Nazi concentration camps he assisted and tended to with his mom, as a teen, in Paris, while his dad was the Canadian ambassador to France.

And again, "the wounded" in a new way, in his thirties, when through his friendship with Father Thomas Phillipe, he became aware of the plight of thousands of people institutionalized with intellectual and developmental disabilities. He responded by inviting two such men, Raphael Simi and Phillipe Seux to come live with him. *His* name was Jean Vanier. He died last week. In this home. In France. He was 90, in earth years.

In his wake, there are now 147 such communities in 35 countries on five continents, doing what he did. People with disabilities, and those who assist them, live together in homes and apartments, sharing life with one another and building community as responsible adults. All governed by his belief that people with disabilities are teachers, rather than burdens, *bestowed* on families.

"The secret, he says, "is meeting people, not through the filters of certitude, ideologies, idealism or judgements, but heart to heart; listening to people with their pain, their joy, their hope, their history, listening to their heartbeats."

This whole enterprise is named L'Arche. The ark. Carrying the full and complete load of us, on our way.

Merci Jean.

★　★　★

In the early 70's, I was contacted by the Canadian Broadcasting Corporation, the CBC, and asked to write a score for a brief, 7 minute, biography they were producing to highlight Vanier's life and work. I said, "Who?" And "What work?" And "I'll get back to you."

Within the week, I discovered a world treasure. A learned, heart-centered human, with a selflessness few of us ever see, much less live out or enflesh.

I called back with a resounding yes. And since it was still a work in its initial stages, could I write an opening and closing part with a scene in mind? I could. I chose an opening that pictured one of "the wounded" with a butterfly on his/her finger. And to close with a sequence and a lyric that had already come to me, that gave tribute to the great inclusion of dance he fostered. Ending in a freeze frame, right out of a twirl.

"Waltz me around and hear the sound you know I've got to give."

★　★　★

I called my friend John Pell and asked him if he would take on the arrangement of instrumental sections we would have to have, and have it all time out to the 7 minutes. He said yes, called *his* friend, Billy Puett, a world class flautist, to flesh out (read *multitrack* and *improvise*) the big center section instrumental, and along with strings and keyboard, we were off.

★　★　★

The video project never made it to full production. Fortunately Jean and L'Arche did. We *did* get this song, and the chance to pay tribute to one of the world's least known (how poetic) lovers of us.

Who's in There?

This morning I had an awareness. When I look inside I can't find myself. And then I realize I can't *ever* find myself, because I *AM* myself. And because I'm not two selves, one looking and the other not found. And because I am not lost. Ever. I'm right here. *And* I don't *possess* myself.

This is simultaneously liberating and frightening. Liberating to not be on the hook to "keep me going" and *frightening* to not be on the hook to "keep me going." Who's got this? Teetering on groundlessness and the ambiguity of being human. Resting there if I am able. Empty of definitions or boundaries. Not the mind-made me, or the "me" that has an expiration date.

What am I? Whatever I am is conscious. Or consciousness is what I am. Whatever I am is not exclusive.

Who am I? This suggests a self. I say I am *my*self, though inside I don't have any history or age or gender or race or body even.

Who am I?

Who indeed?

Westward Ho

It was like a sling shot on a long umbilical cord. She was in the Nissan. I was in the van. Heading out West. Head 'em up, move 'em out. Westward ho, the wagons. Two hours ago she took a blue matte-board folding flap from a black-robed kindly president that said she was a Bachelor(ette?) of Fine Arts. A maid of Fine Arts really. Cum laude. That was a surprise to all three of us. The woman at my side in the lead wagon, myself, and this newly invested adult in the Nissan, my daughter.

My daughter. She'll always be that. At least in this lifetime. My child, my young one to parent, she is no longer. With the first city we hit and the I-70s running into the I-57s and the three digit inner belts and outer belts and heavy work traffic, the wagons disappeared and the Andretti's got on board. I, Mario, Joe. Maleita, wife and co-driver (actually another member of the Penske team). And Michelle, Michael—currently drafting and dodging behind Pop, content to give me St. Louis, but Boulder would be hers.

On the Indy cars they have a "spoiler" in back and up front, interchangeable for different style tracks. They act like wings in reverse. They're to hold the car *down* on the track. *Our* spoilers are all *inside* the Voyager and the Pulsar. Sewing machine, costumes, mannequins, batting, bobbins and bolts. Next Friday she's due as a fiber artist, surface designer at Boulder's Summer Shakespearean Festival. At Spring Break she had saved all her coins, went out to Boulder to interview, flashed her portfolio and landed the job. She's in love with the Mountains and the Colorado sky, and vows she will stay there. Her job and her lodging expire in early July. She says she will find a way to stay *and* do her art. I am in awe of her courage. I relate to her drive.

There is not enough room in this van for a sneeze. Her car either. I see her in my side view mirrors. The rear one is a loss. She is listening to something familiar. Probably Don Henley. A tape. She is bouncing and mouthing the words. Her windows are open. Her hair is streaming. Long, beautiful black hair. Who will run his fingers through her long black beautiful hair? And her life? Could he possibly love her as tenderly as I do? It is not mine. It is hers. Boulder is hers.

★　★　★

I am glad we went from room to room before she left. Last time she was home, just after Spring Break, Maleita said she would like some "ritual" to close this part of our lives. We came up with something simple and rich. Go and sit in each room in our house, see what stirs up, and share.

We remembered the zany puppet shows in the den. Her crafty cuisine from her Mickey Mouse cookbook in the kitchen. Her watercolor Matisse's on the back deck. In my office I remembered how many places my work took her and how pleased I was to give the world to her. I told her I was sorry for any short-changedness she might have felt in my tradeoffs between my work and her. Later, in Johnny's old room (he's moved out already) we both could tell her how sorry we were so much of our attention got focused on John's learning disability and how we regretted whatever that might have cost her. In one of the most rewarding moments in all my parenting she said she always sensed there was room for her, and she was special too. I feel proud for my part.

I wish she would get over in this lane behind me. I don't like it when she slingshots out. I-70 is hard enough to stay on through this St. Louis interstate maze. We sandwich a huge semi between us, lose visual contact and our turnoff is *now*. She will miss it. I must stay with her. I swing behind the semi. She *is* on the other side. I signal her and we turn off at the next exit beyond our missed one, to regroup. As we pull off my heart is pounding. I almost lost her. We had no plan.[56] We made no plan on how to find each other if we got separated. I lost her in the graduation crowd several times, too. Thousands of people. Hundreds of cap-and-gowners. Even when they settled in chairs it was hard from a high-side view to see anything but hair. I settled on counting rows and seats so I could return to her any time I needed to during the surprisingly brief, pleasant and reverent ceremony.

The master of ceremonies' opening remark was that *there are many children here today and they will do what young children do. It is our hope there will be no undue concern about their spontaneity or vocalese. This is after all their job and they are the graduates of the future.* I couldn't help but recall the Master Teacher's remarks on the same subject, "Suffer the little children to come to me...of such is the kingdom." I had held Michelle in my arms, heard her squeal with delight, watched her turn a flower around and around in her hands with an ocean of wonder in her eyes, got soaked with her as she splashed all over her nakedness and my clothes in and by a late evening tub, felt her explore every shape, nook and cranny my face had to offer till finally she landed upon my most handsome nose, squeezed it—and thus was born the "Mad Honker." Changed her and dressed her and powdered her. Carried her off to places only big people could go. Stood with her at the edge of the sea. Watched her roar at the waves, then finally let go and jump in. Of such is the kingdom. Not a bad deal.

★   ★   ★

She is not lost. We are re-united in downtown St. Louis. No wonder the traffic is so crazy for a Saturday afternoon, the Cardinals are playing at Busch Stadium. We agree we will not go any further than Columbia tonight, and if we get separated to meet at the first exit in Columbia. It's I-70 all the way.

When she stood up to get her diploma and got in that huge line in Racer Arena, before her name was called and no other parent would likely know who she is, or who *she* is and none of her classmates knew her before Murray State and none of them were going to Boulder, I had a profound sense of being her continuity. I knew her. I loved her. I cared for her life—before, now, and to come. She was not lost out there. I held her with my eyes and my heart. In my darkest, most lost moments I want to believe God is holding me so. Watching out for me and watching out *from* me, without and within—my safe place, my comforter. In the darkest dark I find I believe in mostly the without. The without with hands and a face. God in *your* skin. Not mine.

It is good to get off the road. Helloooo Columbia. Night number one on a three day blitz. Actually a six day blitz. I want to be back by Friday night for my sister's wedding. Today has been full. I am glad we came yesterday to Murray to pack up all the belongings. Graduation and a good chunk of Kentucky and Missouri miles seems sufficient for one twenty four hours.

Today also held a farewell. John had driven over to Murray from Louisville. I am glad it was important for him to be there. My family didn't show up for graduations with any consistency. My Mom and Dad didn't come to my local concerts or lectures. I still find it hard to acknowledge my achievements to myself. I have four degrees in a trunk somewhere in the attic.[57]

Today, after the ceremonies it began to rain. John helped Michelle load the last of things to take to *our* house in his car—he would be heading back to Louisville. I had been shuttling them back and forth to the dorm and to the car with my trusty gargantuan Wilson golf umbrella. It will shelter a small town. Maleita joined us on the last walk and everything was loaded in and Michelle said, "Well good-bye buddy." She and John embraced. A long time. And it rained. And I stood there holding the umbrella and I am flooded, suffused with the beauty of the simple privilege of having with my life put up a shelter for these three—and me—to be safe and eat in, come and go in, embrace in—leave from. I smile. We *are* better off under the umbrella.[58] Hang this one on the wall. Nice job Joe.

★   ★   ★

Day number two. I think I am anticipating getting Michelle closer to her mountains and her new career as much as she is. I look into her face at breakfast. I am not even close. She's alert enough to land the space shuttle or do brain surgery. She has anticipatory, precedent aspenglow. Energy flying everywhere. I am tempted to tell the waitress—*just bring her bread, she'll do her own toast.*

Out on the road I think, *I* am not getting her closer. *She* is. She's driving. But still I sort of am getting her there. And besides, it's not Boulder yet. What it is, is Kansas. What it *is* and what it *is* and what it *is.* There is this great postcard we find and mail to a good friend who used to live in Kansas. It is solid black with a white outline of the state. It says: "Night time in Kansas." For day, I guess you just reverse the colors?

Kansas, a great place for reveries. Even Dorothy knew that. On automatic pilot (cruise control) down eternal I-70, I see Michelle in my mind's eye. She is sixteen and sculpting in a blazing sun by a creek in the mountains at Blackhawk[59]—her first time to do art in Colorado. She is nine and wandering wide-eyed through the Louvre, remarking on Rembrandt's noses, and wondering why Johnny keeps talking about hamburgers. She is five and has just chalked a Winnie the Pooh floating through space on her kindergarten sidewalk, and asks me if we could take it home.

Midday arrives and the relief of eating presents itself. We are in or maybe I should say *at* Dorrance—there's not enough to be *in.* A filling station and a mobile home diner look like the whole deal.

I expect Kansas to have cut deeply into Michelle's enthusiasm. She bounces out of her car like Florence Griffith Joiner—ready to do a 100 meter dash or a commercial, whichever's up next, on the road to the Olympics. "Tomorrow at this time" she announces with a burst I'm afraid will throw Dorrance into molecular rearrangement, "I *will be* on Mountain Time. Heaah!" For a minute I think she is going to high five the old man sitting on the porch.

We order three sandwiches and I try to adjust to the cessation of 65 miles per hour, the maintenance of that speed and energy by

Michelle in conversation, and the minus 65 the o w n e r d o e s i n
p r e p a r i n g o u r l u-u n-n ch-h- h.

*   *   *

Maleita takes on the afternoon Kansas. We keep asking Michelle if
she wants us to spell her in the Nissan. "Nope. I'm fine." She *is*. She
is also twenty two. This 50 year old lets the seat back and pops in
the Kathy Mattea tape he bought three days before the trip. I was
planning the logistics of packing in my head on the way back from
working out at the gym and the AMZ D.J. said, "Here's a new one
from Kathy Mattea." She sang:

> *She came from Fort Worth,*
> *But Fort Worth couldn't hold her.*
> *Her dreams were bigger than the Texas skies.*
> *She's got a one way ticket on the next bus to Boulder*
> *And it won't take long to say good-bye.*[60]

I am glad we have three days to say good-bye. I glance in the mirror
on my side. *She* is singing again. Her *own* song. Sun roof open. Hair
on the fly. Kathy sings:

> *One last look in the mirror*
> *At the girl she used to be…*

Michelle disappears in the blur of my eyes.

In the song she goes to Boulder at the invitation of a kindly
handsome male. I drift back to my office in our room to room good-
bye and hear Michelle talking: "If I get settled with or live with a
man, I'll first want to find out how he is with children. How he
would be when I am sick. Whether there would be room for me *and*
his job. If he would ask me about *my* work." And then she put on
the capper, "He doesn't have to be perfect, but he *must* be amazing."

I settle and try to drift. Even Kansas can't put me to sleep. Tonight, we have decided, we will sleep in Oakley. Named for Annie. Another girl from the East (Darke County Ohio) who headed West. Tonight, Michelle would plot a surprise Mother's Day party for Maleita. Oakley on a Sunday was not exactly a mecca for shopping, but it did hold what Michelle wanted to give her Mom—a plant. How fitting. Maleita gave *her* one five years ago when she first went away to college. It rides atop her pile in the Nissan directly under the sunroof. It's the oldest living continuous friend she's had since she left "home." Both plants are *leafy* plants. No flower blooms. I see Michelle and Maleita as the blooms.

★   ★   ★

Day three. Denver day. Mountain day. Boulder day. As we hit the Colorado border we pull off and we whoop and holler a little, and I get a picture of Michelle standing beneath the beautiful wooden sign that says, "Welcome to Colorado." Alice in Wonderland. Theme of her senior show. She re-created the Mad Hatter's tea party. Alice's dress hugs the head liner in the van. She *is* an Alice. A *let's just see what's behind this door—Oh this looks like fun—I wonder what this does if I pull this—Oh yeah try this on and see what happens* kind of adventuress. I love that in her. Even as I know this is not without *fear,* the element that makes things brave.

Maleita is driving the van through Denver, through Mountain Time. Michelle had tooted when we crossed into Mountain Time— set her watch, shot her arm up through the sun roof, and did a spontaneous wrist dance.

The far side of Denver comes quickly and the first mileage sign to Boulder. We enter a long underpass. Maleita says, "Perfect, a tunnel." As we pull out of it Michelle slingshots out and soars into the lead. I see them both side by side for a moment as she passes. Both with their plants. Yesterday mother's day, today daughter's day.

My inner ear hears an old song from the sixties,

> *Goodbye Michelle my little one...*
> *We had joy we had fun*
> *We had seasons in the sun...*[61]

"My little one." You are not that any longer. You are quite adult. Resourceful. Able to ask for help. Easy with yourself. Tender with the child in you. A friend had just told me, when our children have taught us everything they can, they move on. Thanks, *ma belle. That* you will always be. Michelle, *ma belle*[62]—my beautiful one, and *your* beautiful one. And *now*, the world's.

One last roar, and in you go.

Joe Wise

Parenting/Options

"Don't be a baby."
Or laughing at the child.
Versus
"This can be hard.
It *was* for *me*."

Morning, Noon, and Night

This is from writers group. The prompt is: a small reflection on this time in your day. What pops up. We are long into Covid 19 lockdown.

From my morning, a trip to the track (where I run) just after dawn. Up Aspen, over on 12th, I go past a new sign (or new to *me* maybe) in front of the Methodist Church, "Sermons on Facebook." And I assume some are still on "Sin." I haven't checked in *with* or *on* any organized religion lately. Sermon topics still catch my attention though. One Sunday morning, coming home from the bakery I passed a church's front yard sign board that said, "The End of the World. 11 o'clock."

It was already 10:30.

I'm also remembering a Christmas sermon at a midnight service a few decades back, when I lived in Kentucky. I was commenting on it to the minister outside after church, as we kept shifting our weight in the cold. He said, "There are so many topics to choose from at Christmas, but I figured I couldn't go wrong with 'fear.'" We both laughed. Two puff clouds in the chill.

★ ★ ★

From my midday, a trip to Sedona for a routine doctor's visit. The view is anything *but* routine. It is *Sedona*. I remind myself not to take it for granted. Or for *granite*, for that matter. It's softer and more colorful. And lends itself to more shapes. A lot like my current body.

My new colors come from the sun. And phantom, time-release, how-in-the-world-did-this-happen arm and leg bruises. Did I mention I'm going on 81?[63] My *bod*, not my car. Still within the speed limit. *Way* within. My whole life is.

★   ★   ★

From my evening. My wife, Maleita, has made some curried chicken salad. I love every ingredient. The bell peppers and celery, almond slivers, grapes and *avocado*. Woah! And Keith Morrison has been recorded on Dateline and will present all the elements of a *crime* salad. I love them all as well. But especially the dogged family and cops, the sweet taste of justice, karma, or in its basest form, (some would say its most delicious form), *revenge*. This almost always requires a palette cleanser and dessert. That lately, is "Andy Griffith" and/or "Frasier." Andy for a reminder of man's humanity to man and beginner's mind. And Frasier to grandly mix acculturation and buffoonery. Popping hoity-toity balloons.

★   ★   ★

Like every other day, it is perfect. And I *know* it is (or could know) the second it is *over*. Working on *during*. My reminder is a frequent mental self-addressed postcard saying, "Having a wonderful time. Wish I was here."

Take a Gander

I've given up knowing
What's good for the goose
And similarly
For the gander.

But I know in a tick
Or a trice or a bit
What e'er suits me well
And what up gets my dander.

And my ace in the hole
I'm wiser and know
What the universe deals
Is always much grander.

Bloomington

This is a tale of two cities. *Bloomington* Indiana and *Louisville* Kentucky. It was the best of times. It was the worst of times. Great in its results. Wrenching in its requirements. It involves a Young Knight. No, not that one. Not *Bobby* Knight, the longtime coach. This Knight wasn't from *Bloomington*. He was from *Louisville*, but he went to Indiana University (in Bloomington). As an 8 year old.

★ ★ ★

"He has a minimal brain dysfunction," Dr. Weiskoff said, and I went numb. "We think it may have happened in the womb." There was a long silence in the room. Then…"Would you like a few minutes alone?" Maleita and I nod, and leave the conference room…walk down the corridor…and out onto a balcony in the back of the building. We are alone with our news. Speechless. Speech. The very thing we find our son, John, at age 3, wrestling with. Or at least that was our perception. Not his ability to *speak*, so much as being able to converse. Finding the words. Processing. And then speaking.

After our tears, we begin to find, collect the adult, parental parts of ourselves, the part that says, "This is what is. What can we do?" We make our way back to the conference room where Dr. Weiskoff and his colleagues await us.

"What do you want for John?" he asks.

"Whatever is the widest berth or the most choices he might have in this world."

"We will help you."

★ ★ ★

Thus began the trek. For the four of us. John. His sister, Michelle. And his parents, Joe and Maleita. *And,* thanks to Louisville (as early as 1972) having a full blown "Child Evaluation Center," a place to begin. While Bloomington (at I.U.) with its renowned seminal children's program embedded in its Speech and Audiology Department, gave us, five years later, a place to crescendo.

Maybe in the womb?... Maybe at birth?... After we plumbed the professionals, we let go of *how's* and *why's* and gave full attention to *what. What* is it? And *what* can we do for and with this beautiful soul in our care? The Center *did* help us. With both "*what's.*" I am profoundly grateful we, as a culture, were moving from the understanding and labels of only "normal" and "retarded." John's journey began at a great juncture in science and psychology and education. More refinement. More specification. More willingness to try new things.

He began with a series of programs and people. Some from the Center. Some not. One of his early constants was Dr. Cande Steckol, then director of Speech and Audiology at the University of Louisville. After his first visit, John came back out to us in the waiting room. I asked him, "How was Cande?"

"She was happy to me."

This was the kind of thing John would say often. Something profound and poetically true, but may be cause for not being included or even teased, and beyond, in some circles. One night, at supper, the four of us, as we said grace one at a time, Johnny's offering was, "Help us change into our lives." I still say that one for me. Of course other nights he would thank Lee Holdridge and everybody else, by name and role, for helping Neil Diamond record *Tap Root Manuscript.*

All his favorite artists and their bands and producers eventually made it into his "grace."

This was part of John's paradox. He could (once at the Center) walk past a table full of magazines, glance over, and say, correctly, "Hmm, *Psychology Today.*"

★ ★ ★

It came to be my/our concern: was he going to have to memorize (and he had a *great* one—memory that is) was he going to have to memorize *everything*? Can he connect *this* with other things? Relationally. Deducing things. Forming and "getting" analogies.

A friend of a friend, helped us with this. The friend, a med student, had a friend in his class, specializing in children, pediatrics. Mohan. From India. He came and stayed with us for a few days, and played and interacted with John. The strongest currency for communication between them seemed to be music and sound. I will note here (no pun intended) that I believe John has an almost infinite eidetic aural memory.

In 1971, when *Jesus Christ Superstar* was released on vinyl, I/we were one of the "first in line" in Louisville to purchase it, transport it at *mostly* legal speeds, and fire it on to a ready-as-rain turntable. It was, for me, a *tour de force*. Something so new with something so old. Something so human about something so divine. We finished all four sides. Ate lunch. And started all over again.

That evening we tucked Johnny, now two, almost three years old (and Michelle, four) in for the night, headed to our bedroom, and were just getting into bed ourselves when from his open door down the hall we heard him, Johnny, make sounds, on pitch, identical to the first six notes of the overture. "Unh, unh, uunh. Unh, unh, uunh." I think, *he really liked this.* Then more notes, more sounds, more patterning: dynamic, pianissimo, mezzo forte, harsh, sweet, fluid, staccato. It went on and on. And it started to form in my head, what I was hearing, was *side one*—in sequence. Maleita and I begin to look at each other in wonderment. Then in dis-belief, excitement, fear, and a gathering joy—right through to the end of *side four*.

Johnny was also, by now, traveling everywhere with a spindle of 45s (an ancient iteration of vinyl recordings allowing independent housing for "singles"). Stuffed animals, or even portions of a favorite blanket, held no attraction for John. The records were his comfort and companions, in the bascart, in the back seat, in the playroom, in the pew. Often spinning the top one and singing it. Words were coming.

With Mohan, John could share the U.S. top 40, and he could hear in return the sitar and tabla-rich music of ancient and modern India. At the end of his stay, Mohan concluded Johnny *was making* inferences and connections and analogies in his mind.

★　★　★

The Center's team and work, especially with Dr. Bloom (yes that's his name) confirmed this capacity in the Young Knight, jousting with elements of comprehension, wordage, discourse and conversation, while maintaining a clear heart and an unflinching hold on the joys of childhood. He had everything but bugs on his teeth from riding his Big Wheel. Swings and things on playgrounds, were among his essentials.

My own favorite moments with young John, include this one, right at the top: Brushing my teeth. With *his* coaching. Basically two directives, both related to speed. He would say "slow" and I would droop my body and sag my face and move my brush at an infinitesimal pace until he said "fast." Whereupon I would brighten my face and do a little jig while moving my head and my brush all about, all at something approaching, oh… Mach 1. He would laugh till he dropped. And could stop laughing long enough to say "slo-ow." We continued until *I* dropped, from exhaustion.

Along with unusual, for lack of a better term, aural memory, John was coming up similarly in the visual department. Once he asked

Maleita if she remembered Sharon bringing him some Cheerios at breakfast. Maleita said, "Where?"

"In Valdosta, Georgia."

"Oh yes, last *year?*... On *vacation?*... At a *restaurant?*... How do you know her name?"

Pointing to his heart he said, "It was right here." (Her waitress plaque.)

This is a truism for John, even to this day. If he meets you, you will be remembered (and known by heart).

Fortunately for John, and all of us, there were schools, places of learning in Louisville, up and running, that sought to honor different modalities, different *pathways* of learning. In these, he would form singular bonds with a teacher or two, and he would foster and continue that relationship for decades, in all cases, until the teacher/friend passed.

★   ★   ★

In the beginning of John's 9th year, Maleita and I got a call from the Child Evaluation Center requesting a conference with their staff. "Yes, of course." It sounded like more than an update. We were curious, excited even. John seemed to be progressing, but we knew we were too close for a reliable, solidly *objective* evaluation.

Dr. Weiskoff opened with, "There is increasing evidence that communication skills in childhood find their most conducive landscape at age 8." *Ok?* "It also seems to be the last chance for a significant *growth spurt* in that department." *Ok?* "So we have a recommendation for John." *Ok!* "There are two programs in the country that specialize in fleshing out this well studied hypothesis." *Yes!* "Logopedics in Kansas City, and Indiana University at Bloomington." *Are we gonna have to move?* No sooner had I thought this, than he said, "It's a *residency* program."

"Residency?"

"By design. It's a significant factor in its successes."

Whoa! Where do we start? Emotionally? Physically? Practically? Details.

We contact Indiana University. We meet Dorothy Salzman, Department Head and Program Director of this nascent, hopeful learning path. We come home with 3 big takeaways. 1) We really like Dr. Dorothy. 2) John comes home on weekends. 3) It is geographically, distance-wise, easily do-able.

Then, there were the *other* do-ables. Can we, can *I* do this? It felt so at the far end, the diminishing end of "parental" and "fostering," landing more on an "abandonment" scale. And *that*, at some immeasurable amount. The challenge was so deep, and personal, Maleita and I had no ready "help" for each other. I remember, when the pain and overwhelm began to take over, my going to see, a friend of a friend, Art. An acquaintance, I was about to become as vulnerable with, as anybody in my life, up to this point.

Art had a son he had sent, released, gave, there is no precise word for this ("surrendered-with-hope" comes closest)—he had *entrusted* his child to an out of town residency program for "extreme hearing impairment" some time before I met him. He agreed to see me on an "emergency" basis. He owned a pharmacy in a medical building. He told his assistant to cover for him and he took me back to the last row, between the stacks, like a library, the last row, of all the medicines. We sat on two crates. And he became the balm, the salve, the relief nothing in all these rows could offer me.

I said all my "How did you's?"

He said all his "I don't know's."

He put his arm around my shoulder while I released my dam.

I left drained. And full. And *perhaps*...ready?

★　★　★

We set out on our second trip to Bloomington. John is on board. It is the beginning of summer. The program he is now enrolled in is a six week one. To see if he, and we, and the team at I.U. can do this. Will it be a fit all the way around? Will we all move on to a Fall and

Spring semester, a school year? I don't remember much about that journey up into that beautiful woodsy part of Indiana, other than noticing (I had missed it the first time) on close to the last bend in State Route 38 before we enter Bloomington, there is a large stand-alone John Deere sign—greeting us as we bring our Dear John to his work, his cultivation, his tasks.

After getting him settled in his dorm, we find our way to the playground, and play like we are playing. I believe that includes all four of us. Two parents and a sister and a Young Knight. It was *he* who eventually called us out of the dread and into the moment. "Well Mom and Dad, I have to go to work." And he turned from the swing set and walked alone toward the building and people that were his new "home." (I can't say I've seen a braver act in my life.)

And we began what would become our routine for a year. Get into the car. Whoever was crying the least would drive. Stop at the phone booth about a half hour down the road (1977. No cellphones). Talk to the den mother at the dorm. She would say, "He cried for a while, but now he's engaged in the playroom with the others." Momentary relief, then back to the shock of the new "normal."

Looking back I believe he was always more *engaged* in the playroom than any of us traveling the new, now lonely, road to our physical home. During this time, I now see, it was hard to access empathy for anyone. I felt like I had little emotional room for anyone or any*thing* else.

My work? It needed to go on. Beyond the drive I felt in the calling to do it, it now became fiscally necessary in an up tempo way. Accept more bookings. Travel out more frequently. The original design I was able to carry out, with the blessings of invitations, was to have me at work on the road on the weekends, and at home during the week. The schedule that allowed me to do all the things with Michelle and John that a 9 to 5 father had to miss. That schedule now would dramatically limit my time with John. We tried a couple of times, the I.U. team and I, scheduling *me* an afternoon, solo, midweek, with John in Bloomington. It quickly proved too disruptive to everybody but *me*. I got some relief for seeing him, by getting home for more Sundays. It was just a hard time for all of us.

★   ★   ★

Johnny's program was intensive and amazing. Intensive in scope and saturation. Amazing in its dynamic design. "John's working on prepositions this week," the clarion call went out. The Dorm Mother, the grad students who saw him in individual sessions, the teacher and afternoon classes he was mainstreamed into at a school in town, the bus driver who took him to and fro, and of course a host of departmental professional staff, *all* knew John was working on prepositions this week, and would engage him in conversation geared to highlight prepositions, all accenting a *specific* one each day. Today's word is "with."

The teacher at the local school, told all her students, it was like John was from Mars and was learning how to speak on Earth, and they could welcome him and help him. They did. They all did. They were "with" him. All the way.

The "residency" part of this we soon saw was, among other things, to heighten the effect of John's being unable to make sounds or gestures or phrasings he was comfortable with, and we were "complicit in," at home. But, at this point, *no one* was starting from scratch. In-home "schooling," especially with Maleita, and a family of blood and friendships were tuned in and helping out before, during and after this current sojourn.

John had a way of attracting to himself people who wanted to foster and help him with their skills. And love him. And then be taken in by him.

Dr. Dorothy and her husband Irv would call us and say/ask, could they take him home to their house for dinner. Judy Kelly, in one of the special needs schools John had already attended, had coaxed him through several break-throughs, including an "I want that truck!" moment with another child. She called him throughout his childhood to see how he was doing, until he got old enough to call *her* and see how *she* was doing. Still does. In his favorite school, Meredith-Dunn, a private program geared for the individual needs of different learning paths, in Louisville, post Bloomington, John met, was taught by, and the rest of that dance, Jane Ratterman and Sherry Wilson. Sherry, his all-time *favorite*. Maybe a tie with Cande Steckol.

And this might be a good time to share a special encounter John had with Dr. Steckol. We were taking him to his weekly session with her, in her office building in Louisville, and it turned out to be on his birthday. A little before the hour was up, she came out alone and was weeping, *laughing*, trying to compose herself, laughing, stopping herself, laughing, and trying to get settled enough to speak. We have no idea what this could mean.

"*I...I...gave John this hat*...(laughter, starting up again). (A snap-down flat-sloped cap with U of L emblazoned on the bill). *And he* (laughing)... *he said* (as she settled herself) *he said in a calm but decisive tone...'Cande, I hate this hat'*...(laughter, long, for us all)...'*It's for old men*'...(down to a smile)... *I like T-shirts.*'" The box and wrapping were in shreds in her other hand.

No guessing with John.

He called *her*, till she passed. Even though she was hired away, to head their Communicative Disorders Department, by the University of Alabama. And Dr. Dorothy, till *she* passed. And Sherry Wilson, sudden and young, an aneurism, in *her* passing, having just been named Louisville's teacher of the year.

★   ★   ★

Bloomington was drawing down. Spring semester was drawing to a close. Dorothy and Irv invite us all, the Young Knight and his family, to their favorite Japanese restaurant for dinner. I couldn't feel it as a time to celebrate, with so many other unknowns in John's ongoing development. Definite progress was evident. Was it enough? Would it ever be? How much of what he picked up here was transferable? To a new as yet unplowed field? Could I let go of my "enough's?" It was easy to see why he loved Dorothy and Irv. The time with them, *did* give us a chance to see how connected we *all* were, to the soul we know as Johnny.

School-wise he still had more to go. All in Louisville. Meredith-Dunn, Chenoweth Public School, Trinity High School, and Sullivan Junior College. Each step a giant one, over steep crevices. At the outset no one could say where his wings were capable of taking him. Or not.

It was a blessing that no one ever told John anything about any of that. Anywhere along the way.

He told *us, Bloomington* was a smash. One morning, in the kitchen, when he was 17. Right before his high school graduation. Right after he came home and announced he had a job at Winn-Dixie supermarket. (We had no idea he was looking.) A year before he moved out into his own apartment. With a full time job. "You remember taking me to Bloomington? That was the best thing for me. It made me able to do all my many things."

How many parents get that? Not just the gratitude. But out loud. In words. We felt lucky. And blessed.

John has "Bloomed," Bloomington bloomed, *is* blooming everywhere he goes. Phoenix, a half a year before Maleita and I moved to Sedona. Nashville (making this a tale of 3 now 4 cities) Nashville while *we* stayed in Arizona. 1800 miles away. Independent in every category. *Inter*dependent in all the ways any of us would do well to emulate. John doesn't have a phone tree, he is a one man phone-forest. His bloom, in *my* eyes, glows with heart-centered clarity, embraces its own uniqueness, and stands in steadfast fidelity, to and with, those it knows in the garden.

My Son, in whom I am well pleased. And well blessed.

★   ★   ★

Nashville. Music City. Of *course* it's where John lives. John has, always has had, a parallel symbiotic life with music.

He told us he heard the Beatles in the womb. He told us at age 6 the Paris Subway's arriving signal was b flat. Yes, he has perfect pitch.

He, as a young teen, could and did tune all the stringed instruments in a 12 piece band with no reference to the Steinway. Or to each other. Pacman, the video game, he once observed in a busy arcade, was in E minor. All this, while he says of a mercilessly off-pitch participant at a local karaoke bar (right before it was *his* turn) after we asked, if that hurt to hear—John's response, "He's really having a good time."

In his 10th year, John came upstairs, before breakfast, and asked if he could play my guitar.

"Sure." This is his first venture past air guitar. He played his way through "Lights of the City."[64] Astonished, I asked him how he knew how to play that? Meaning, the guitar.

He said, "I watched Ed's fingers last night (Ed Gutfreund) on that song. I dreamed I could play it."

I had been waiting for *him* to express any interest in playing. He eventually had a couple of teachers who ran out of things to teach him, then found a couple who really engaged him, and by the time he began to play with *me*, on the road, in his early teens, he was by far the more accomplished player in *our* duo.

In high school, after choral practice, the music teacher asked him if he would play a solo in the upcoming talent show. "Sure." J.S. Bach's "Bourree in E minor."[65] Fittingly on classical guitar. Maleita asked him if he was nervous. "No, I've played with Dad."

When he began doing stage work, other than with me, I'd asked him the same question, and he would say, "unnnh…maybe 5%." *My* butterflies couldn't even get two flaps at 5%. Though fortunately they'd all settle in after I started.

I see him as an 8 year old, at 3:00 a.m. in Columbia Studios, Nashville, singing and recording his first solo ("Show Me Your Smile").[66] The rest of us on session were in the control room listening. One take. We all clapped. He said, from his perch on the giant stool, head swallowed in the "huge" headset, "No, only clap when it is *live* in concert, not in the studio." It didn't dampen us a bit.

I see him at family gatherings, playing Rock and Roll Trivia and telling everybody, "C'mon, *you* know this." While he ran the table.

It's too bad the game didn't ask musician's birthdays or some such, to keep him *more* interested. Actually something *beyond* the birthdays or death days. He knows so many. Some tied to his own event–life. Glen Frey of the Eagles, died on the same day in the same year as Sherry Wilson, his "all time teacher."

I see him in a living room concert, at our house in Sedona, taking requests after his "program," and an elder asked him if he knew "Over the Rainbow." He said, "Wait a minute," closed his eyes for a little while, opened them and said "Yes." He played and sang it beautifully. After everybody went home, I asked him if he'd ever played that song. He said simply "No." I remember "*Superstar.*" And "Lights of the City."

I see him at the Rudyard Kipling, a great place for musicians in 1980's Louisville, doing a solo show for the first time. All the adults who had touched his life and he theirs, showed up. Teachers. His YMCA Youth Soccer coach (Giampaolo Bianconcini). Soccer coach's son and teammate (Luca) who John is still close with. Music teachers. His Mom and Dad's friends, who had followed and fostered him as well. Family. And "family."

I remember Bloomington, his *first* solo, in *life*. And the brave path he has walked since. *Is* walking. Landing in his favorite place from childhood, Nashville. Also home to his favorite musician, friend, travel buddy, "uncle?" John Pell, affectionately, after concert trips to Hawaii, known as Big Keoni,[67] while he was still a young, Little Keoni. Nashville. Working "sound jobs" along the way. In audio/ visual production studios and sound duplication companies. Steady food delivery as second job. Things that nourish the body. And the soul.

That's John, up till now.

As with our own lives, we stay tuned.

Even if we don't have perfect pitch.

We can have a good time.

A Delicate Thing

It is such a delicate thing,
To not take myself too seriously
And yet seriously enough
To not trivialize who I am
And the stakes,
The preciousness
Of a human
Life.

We lose *trust* in ourselves
After enough trivializing,
From inside
Or out.

What Keeps Me from Peace?

What keeps me from peace? Stillness? The confidence that all is as it "should be?" The relaxation that starts in my chest and radiates out to the toes and scalp?

Ten times out of ten it seems it's my mind. Swivet-ing on something in the past or firing away at something in the future I'd like to shape a certain way. When it stays in the now, when *I tell it* to stay in the now, and I "activate" my observer self (really *notice*) peace appears. My natural state emerges. *I* am in charge. Not my mind.

When Jesus said, "The Kingdom of God is within you," I think it had to do with this. The "I" of me that is consciousness and in charge of my mind and actions. The saints and mystics in Jesus' tradition affirm this truth. The Kingdom of God is within us. Joel Goldsmith,[68] when speaking of Jesus saying "I and the Father are one," says the "I" of me and the "I" of you and the "I" of the Father are one.

The mind can keep me so easily from this awareness by its dazzling powers. It's by far the most awesome tool in our box, and it's easy to confuse it, because it *is* so powerful, with the "I," or the Consciousness that *is* in charge. Many have said of the mind, "a wonderful servant, a terrible master."

Sometimes in the middle of painting a piece, sanding a board, writing a poem, walking a path, shooting a 20th free throw, my mind goes away and peace appears. My oneness with the Divine (whether I call it this or not) becomes possible to notice.

Much more often it seems, *and* I can change this, I have a sense of separation from the Divine. Often in the past I have paid attention to or at times even inadvertently been part of "creating" crises, mostly I guess because it was *familiar* to me. A strange "comfort." I grew up pretty hypervigilant. In my house the slightest miss-step could, might, cause great wrath. My Church wasn't too much friendlier. I remember in the seventh grade thinking I could go to hell for thinking of Judy Senn's breasts. Slight step for my 12 year old hormones. Great wrath and eternal separation from God for my soul.

Much of my waking time became focused on avoiding miss-steps, not on consciously seeking union with my family or God.

There was a weird comfort in it. At least with the Church. I knew exactly what to do and not do, to belong, to be blessed. At home I was still guessing some, but a lot of it was clear. This and this usually means provoking extreme anger, and this and this usually doesn't. *Just tell me the rules* of course flies in the face of maturity, which I now define as taking charge of my own life. And spiritual maturity as taking charge of my own path.

With guidance, sure. With reference to the past and tradition, sure—but *bound* by neither of these when my tuning fork, my heart, says "no." "This is not a fit." "Not helpful for you." I like that I have something new and useful to put my vigilance skills to. I like that I'm brave enough to take this chance. I like that I am focusing on *my* communion with the Divine, God–in here, and not leaving that to the saints and mystics, while I settle for trying *not* to think of anybody's breasts. Effectively missing out on both gifts.

God-*out*-there is a good way to describe my early spiritual path. God-*in*-here, experienced as "in-here," not separate, my current path. What I see, hear and feel of the Divine "out there" I now take as a mirror of the Divine within.[69]

Many of the mystics speak of hide and seek with God—not as God's cruelty, but as our game. *Lela.*[70] We are always inseparable from the Divine. It is our essence, our true nature. We take on a body, a life, a human story. It has a lot of peek-a-boos, hide and seeks in it.

We drop the body, the truth re-appears as it has always been. I and The Father/Mother are One. Always. All ways.

For the most part I believe we create or focus on crises for the familiarity of it. A strange comfort in its drama.

Living in the now, as it presents itself, has an unscripted, brave, risky part to it that doesn't advertise well—though I like how alive and centered and peaceful I feel when I dare do it.

And there is one practice I recommend to me (teaching what I need to learn) and to you. As things and people and events move into our focus fields, especially if they're loaded with conflict, aggravation, chaos and dis-ease—step back on the inside and say "to whom is this coming?" It puts in focus the truth of our experience which is that *this*, whatever *this* is, is something that comes and goes. Both the situation *and* my thoughts and feelings about it—they all come and go. The "I" of me to whom they come does not come and go. It places the stability and security and ease we all hunger for, with an experience we can repeatedly test and find to be true, in an abiding Presence, untouchable by birth or death,[71] inseparable from the Divine—always. All ways.

4045

4045
That's my lucky number
My lotto number
The PLU #
For nature's jackpot:
Cherries!
Gifting me only
Twice a year,
A seasonal
Offering even
World wide
Produce shipping
Can't rectify.
It feels unfair.
It sucks.
It's just the pits.[72]

(A sweet lesson
In patience
And letting the other tastes
Have their day?)?

Waiting

Of Slings and Marrows

I am waiting for this cast to be off,
Waiting to cast it away
And be under my own management
After my not mal-aligned
Bones do their magic
And re-join, re-connect
With each other.

After a life time of sports
With some sprains, and strains
And tears, the first
Bone in my body,
A tiny, almost missed
On x-ray
Wrist bone
Fractures.
At age 80.

I am cognizant of so many
Friends, my age, peers,
With dramatically different
Results from an impact.
Of course I chose

a collision with the biggest of the bigs—
the earth.
We had a sudden
Unexpected meeting
Last Monday.

I gave up running
On trails a while back
Because of "hidden"
(in the dust) rocks and roots.
My encounter with the globe
Occurred on my longtime
Safe path
Mingus High School's
Running track,
Paved with good intentions
And joint-friendly materials
Especially for an elderly body.
There is nothing
To trip you up,
Or fall you down
Except…
For the carpet runners
For the teams to enter the
Football/soccer field
From side to center.

They appear before and after events,
The carpets.
They are light enough
To be momentarily moved by the wind,
Or better, *bunched* by the wind
In odd random ways—
This phenomenon,
Along with a surprise "appearance"

By a friend and track buddy—"Oh-hi!"
And my own vulnerability
In walking backwards
As usual
On my final lap
To even out my muscles.
This all led to my earth encounter.

And a re-arrangement
Of almost everything else
In my life—though most of it
Is with what I would
Ordinarily call small things
Like opening a jar.
And were this my other wrist
A "big" thing
Which would leave me
Without this pen,
And a soul connection
Like no other.

So, a splint
For a sprint
(Or walking backwards)?

C'mon 2 months
You can sprint.

*   *   *

It was my triquetrum, the fracture. A tiny but necessary contributor to how I fluidly handle the world. Known only *to* and *by* wrist doctors, I dare say. I bet it's kept many a med student from an A+ on *anatomy and physiology* quizzes.

It was big and mighty enough to swell my whole hand, mostly the back of it, plus *all* the fingers. *And* its necessary ingredients and process for healing lets it be a painter. All kinds of reds and purples—all the way to the fingertips, and oddly, at least to me, leaves all my fingernails—bright white. Maybe it's just the contrast. My Orthopede tells me next week my color scheme features green. If the swelling doesn't go down significantly by then, I'll look like I'm carrying four pickles and a gherkin—at the end of this contraption that goes all the way from the forearm onto my hand (and palm) with a porthole for the gherkin.

Like any runner I know, the first thing I wanted to know was when can I get back out and challenge those rugs (and my attention) again. When the splint/cast up to my elbow is changed to a shorter, removable wrist stabilizer, turns out to be the answer.

The PA, I saw, who I suspect is a runner, certainly an athlete, as well as a medical nerd (my favorite kind of "healer") describes and demonstrates how the down fling of an arm in a normal stride will impact the blood and "juice" flow to that area. If all else is going well at that point I need only walk or pause while holding that arm up over my head for a while to let things balance out. And I am released unto my own recognizance. As a friend of mine's child would say, because he couldn't articulate "hallelujah"—"Honolulu!"

This whole incident timed itself poorly calendar wise. December. Good news, I'm in Arizona. Not so good news, it's almost Christmas. How will I unwrap my presents?

★   ★   ★

Oh, but I *do* have this little ditty, send up, if you will, making its way through my consciousness ever' now and again:

All I want for Christmas
Is my left arm back
My left arm back
Yeah, left arm back

Gee if I could only have
My left arm back
Then I could clap
For baby Jesus.

All I *need* for Christmas
Is my good right hand
My good right hand
Yeah, my good right hand
'Cause as long as I can have
My good right hand
I can one hand clap
For baby Buddha...
(can you hear it?)
And baby Jesus...
And baby anybody...
And all my presents...

★   ★   ★

The triquetrum, I discover, is part of a complex kaleidoscope of bones and sinews, tendons and muscles (some morphing into otherness, some even involved in sheathing) a kaleidoscope of players ready for concerted action—that make up the front paws we humans call our hands. Its design allows for the tenderest caress, as well as the mightiest blow. And in the in-between, lies writing, painting, guitar playing, all three of which I've been blessed by on this trip.

★   ★   ★

My two favorite rehab milestones: showering without a plastic bag taped over my left forearm and hand, *and* returning to the track, albeit in December, with some morning's wind-chill factors only in the high teens. Somewhat unusual in my 25 years here in Arizona. So I joined the unusualness with my response. My new wrist brace/

cuff allows for more of my fingers and thumb to see daylight, or day-frost, so a conventional glove was off the table, and off hand, and just off. My cuff is black, and happenstances had just released a less worn, as well as a well-worn mate, in a set of footwear *my* mate, Maleita is discarding. It is a black soft sole slipper—sometimes slipping slowly south—till I hike it up to the Velcro on the brace.

It makes for a quite noticeable extension of that limb. I/we, me and my limb, take to the track. Pumping along. Full stride. Just me and the morning winged ones. And as I round into the middle of my third turn, I look up to the (Mingus) Marauder/pirate looming ever large on the scoreboard, with a blade in his teeth and a fierceness in his eyes—I become fully aware of and affirm—*I still belong to this whole venture we call life...and,* I am Captain Hook's lesser known, softer cousin: Captain Slipper.

"Ahoy ye Ravens!"

Did I hear...? Can a bird...chuckle?"

Going South

A Self Teaching

When things start going south
go with them.
Stay with the "things"
and the "southness."
Most likely this all started
in your head, your mind,
and if it has found no other way,
go with it.
Go south, to the heart, your core,
your *cor.*
There you have more
tools, more balance,
more choices about
responses. Connections with
the Dept. of the Interior
and the Dept. of the Exterior,
should *that* be involved.

The heart has no censor
all feelings are allowed
even shame
welcomed, engaged in/with—
a heart to heart "knowing"

in the safest room
in the house.

The head is busy
the heart is calm.
The head is Martha
the heart is Mary.
You are both.
Know them both.
Honor them both.

Joe Wise

Hop to It

Well it's grasshopper season here at Mingus Mesa. Mingus being the high school here in Cottonwood, Arizona. And "mesa" being the "table" constituted by the track and field here. It's grasshopper season, of course, for the grasshoppers. But it's also the season for ants who apparently *hunt* grasshopper, specifically grasshopper wing. In an eerie elephant tusk kind of way? I don't know. But it took me a few laps to recognize what I was seeing. An upright, solo, perpendicular-to-the-ground grasshopper wing moving slowly across the track toward the dirt apron.

When I saw the second one I stopped and squatted and determined their/its source of mobility was an ant, roughly 1/100th the size of its cargo and prancing merrily along. My first thought was, "Hey, who doesn't love to wind surf?" But the pace never changed. Even in moderate wind gusts.

Whatever was this about? Is this a trophy? Maybe an Ace Hardware solution for an infrastructure challenge at the local ant hill construction site? Or maybe, it was a rare delicacy, like truffles, that some few enlightened multi-skilled haute cuisine brothers and sisters were hip to and capable of harvesting. If that's what it was, then "harvesting" would be the proper term, since this was basically road kill or *track* kill in this case, resulting from some few accidental human and mechanical interactions with these hopper/flyer athletes.

I bet they'd fare well in the Spring/Summer track meets here if they could be lined up at the starting board bound for the triple jump pit, the last leg or action of which would permit the deployment of wings.

I was too time-constrained, needing to be off the track before the "kids," students, arrived and had need of the area, too tight on time to see where the wings were going. If they were going "back to the farm," how in the world would the bearers collapse them enough to get through the typical door/hole into the colony?

I made a mental note to get here early next time to see how this spun out, and just as quickly erased it from the dry board I fancy as a brain, so I could live with whatever fiction I decided.

I went for a "cookout." Like Buffalo wings. Cook out, since it wouldn't fit through the doors and tunnels of the feasters abode. These would all take place at night, when no humans were likely to appear and interfere. A bonfire, after a hard day's work and each camper calling out their order to the resident chefs, with at least one, who would break into the night's stillness and spaciousness with both an *order* and a *tribute* to the great Mr. Miyagi,[73] "Well done, Grasshopper!"

★   ★   ★

During the stretch of summer I observed these phenomena, NPR was reporting on a massive grasshopper "invasion" of Las Vegas and how it was contributing to a decreasing volume of visitors. A member of the Chamber of Commerce was being interviewed, and he went on and on about how it was no big deal and that in fact the *Chinese* considered the grasshopper a bringer of good luck. I'm not sure I would have bought it, but I'd met a couple of ants who would.

The Stars We Are Given

Writer's group. Zoom. Topic (and prompt) taken from a quote in Rebecca Solnit's Storming the Gates of Paradise: *"The stars we are given, the constellations we make." 15 minutes.*

What are my stars? What lights my way, especially in the dark? What winks, even in the black hole? Something (or *no*-thing) I didn't make, but I somehow am, and can never cease to be. In the matrix shines the gifts. The body I walk the planet with. The eyes that see in the day. And night. Magnificent sensors of all stripes.

Eyes-closed knowing. Other beings to travel with. Some of my conscious choosing. This may be my brightest star—"Choice." "Expression"—the next focal point on my Orion's belt. Others gather to me, with me. We wield the sword. The poets and prophets, writers awake in the dark. Cutting through to Truth.

And finding *it is us.* (And we are *it.*)

The Eyes Have It

Begun in writers group. Topic: eyes. 20 minutes.

The eyes have it.
Windows of the soul.
They're all we have now.
It's down to the eyes.
The virus took away the rest of our faces.
  and left us with only
  our soul windows.

To clear the decks for equality?
To really see each other?
  and see *how* we see each other
  and deal with all our subtle
  and not so subtle pre-programming?

The chance to see each other's souls and Spirit.
To see our selves
  In Technicolor, multicolor,
  Full spectrum shades and tones.
To "sing of what we share
  And celebrate our differences."[74]

We can't un-see what we saw.
We can attempt to on a conscious level.

My white, caucasion, mostly European ancestry,
My two eyes,
>   Saw George Floyd
>   Saw Ahmaud Aubrey
>   And Rayshard Brooks
>   Breonna...

We, *our* eyes saw
(even if we weren't there)
>   The wall of unidentified enforcers
>   And the horses as pushers
>   And the pepper spray bullets
>   Helicopter, flash bangs
Clearing the way for one of us
To create a way to be seen.
Moving a peaceful protest
For an optic, a photo op.

Clearer we see,
All lives matter
When black lives matter
And brown lives
Red lives and yellow lives
Matter.

And the eyes *do* have it.
The gift and the blessing
To behold and to send to my soul
The luminous beauty of each and all.

I am grateful.

A Little Perspective

This title is a sub-heading from a chapter in Elizabeth Gilbert's book, Big Magic. *I chose it as a prompt for writers group. Zoom. 20 minutes.*

What a great reminder. Be little again. "I awake as a child to see the world begin," John Denver reminds us in his "Today is the first day, of the rest of my life."[75] What do I *get* to do today, see today, be still with today?

When my friend, Ed Campana, came to visit with us, with his family, our house filled up, adding he and Meredith and three little ones to Maleita and I and our two little ones. Outnumbered we were, the big ones. First morning at breakfast, Ed, the cook, is preparing everybody's meal. Matthew, his son, is served first and back to the range goes Ed.

Mathew becomes vocal about his offering, "I hate eggs. I don't want this egg." Ed, puts down his spatula, walks over and puts a hand on the young one's shoulder and says, "Now Mathew, how do you think that makes the egg feel?" Whereupon Young Mathew, overcome I assume by compassion for the egg, got right into his part of their relationship. Being a consumer.

This was both funny and beautiful to me. The adult became "little" enough to—encourage, teach, coax in a language Mathew seemed to "get." Or maybe it was like the kid who asked so many "whys," *his* Dad finally came up with, "because it's Thursday."

Where we see from is crucial. I see best when I see the *big* picture, with a *"little"* perspective.

Particle or Wave

Writer's group. Zoom. Presented with four images. A chimp, an elephant, empty rickshaw, and a woman holding an eyes-closed infant. Quantum physics informed my reflections, hence the title I've given the piece.

Particle or wave.

Monkey mind or elephant still.

Passengerless taxi or mother-tucked stillness.

"Wisdom tells me I am nothing. Love tells me I am everything. Between the two my life flows."[76]

The pandemic is sure skewing this flow we have known as life. Instead of this being a track meet, with all kinds of events, it mostly feels like never quite having an event. I'm in the starter's block and stuck at "On your marks." Some days I want to just tackle the starter and fire his gun. Get us going. Get me going.

Still, I do get to "dash" about, twice a week, to the grocery aisles, my actual masked, hand-and-cart-sanitized-self more like a stock car racer flying around, minimizing my time, head jerking constantly in 3 directions: ahead for people, up for product, and down for "one ways."

In the heat of this heat, I long for the stillness of the couch, even as I know I'm "holding on" to either a particle or a wave.

Unexpected Gifts in Covid Days

Writers group. Zoom. Maleita's prompt for us. 25 minutes.

Finding an extra pair of socks—moving laundry day off till tomorrow. Watching Adrian Monk find one more thing in his lexicon of anxieties. Discovering, as a writer, or in conversation, just the right phrase to say what you are saying. Seeing *everyone* in Safeway with a mask, and making it truly a safe or safer way. Missing your raven friend early morning at the track, only to find his cousin in the parking lot at Walmart.

Having a long time (25 years) barber *give* you your last haircut before he retires. Knowing he sees our smiles through the opaque masks. As we do his. All of us knowing with our meeting, it was always way more than the haircut.

Finding an extra peach yogurt behind the milk in a late night frig raid.

Getting the out-of-the-blue downtime call from your granddaughter, 79 days before her high school graduation, who just wants to share with you how strange she feels between the sadness of childhood disappearing, while also experiencing the flood of excitement about having an adult life.

Having unexpected, always welcomed, chest releases in the "flow" of stillness. *Feeling* the borderline state between taking a nap and having it take you.

Believing at some level, our communion with Light, Truth, God is limited only by our willingness and desire to awaken, to receive, and our fear of being overwhelmed—for as long as we move around, hanging out, in this flesh. "Practicing?" for the overwhelm?

Surf's Up

From Writer's group. All wrote from this title.

Shoe's off. Shirt's off. Surf's up.

As tender as my feet have become, this sand is such a massage, allowing my full relaxed weight settle with each step.

Aloha feet. Aloha soul.

Here you are to give the same permission to your creative self. Picture this. Picture that. Describe this. Narrate that. Symbol this. Suggest that. All with paper, pigments, canvas, brush. And your free-from-everything-else self.

Possibles are as far as this oceanic horizon.

Thank you. Thank you. Thank you.

Meditation

Meditation.
>Finding out you haven't left
>Where you want to go.

You've arrived
>Before you've departed.

Or it puts you
>In the most likely mode
>For this realization.

Tele-Treasure

When the disconnect began
        between reality and our "rulers"
        between science and our governance
        between truth and self-aggrandizement
        between hope and unmitigated confusion,
Who would ever have thought
That a little-known sometimes-visitor
To the old Keith Olbermann show,
Would become our
        beacon and harbor
        analyzer and heart
        synthesizer and eyes,
Compassionate hostess
Of our fire-side, soul-side
Chats.

Thank you Rachel.
For being you.
For us.

P.S. May the fishing gods be blatantly biased in your favor.

Penultimate

Penultimate.

I love this word. I hate this word. I like a new way to say "next to last" or "second to last." I *don't* like to say or think *anything* about last.

Penultimate. I love the sound of it. I don't like the meaning of it. The suggested, nay *proclaimed* reality of it: "last" is not far behind. It's next. Well, maybe "last toothache" or "last congressional gridlock" or "last dinner with cellphones." And actually penultimate *could* mean hope for "all my trials, soon be over."

This all got pumped up good in me be the accretion of several decades of earth years. The body, the experiences, both shrinking. But it's not *all* bad news. I'm glad to let go of my penultimate eyes. New lenses with my cataract procedures. Back to 20/20. Back to rich reds, blinding whites, and deep blues and purples. I was glad to let go of my penultimate lumbar 4 on the left side. Had several things in there freezing my back up and shutting mobile-me down. Thanks to my lucky stars, I got one of the pioneers of that kind of microsurgery to remove the unneeded culprits in there. I believe I was his penultimate patient. He's retired now. Me and my running and overall mobility are not.

I haven't played golf for a good while, for various unphysical reasons, but when I did, I began to notice I'd get inexplicably anxious on the 17th tee. This, even though, there was always the clear possibility of positing the "reality" of the *19th* hole. Which every golfer knows as the after-round round of rounds in the clubhouse.

Thus postponing the punishing penultimate pulsations till the *18th* hole. I often played on courses with signs on the tees allotted to various advertisers. One such course's 17th hole was sponsored by Williams Funeral Home. Blind-sided.

The third quarter. Lap 19 of my 20 at the track. The second to last bite of my bowl of Breyers, of my all-too-rare, well-done (in every way) In & Out burger. This, even though I'm already *way below* the satisfaction and pleasure level of the *first* two bites of either. We've tried, it seems, to compensate for this factor, in the grand displays of pyrotechnics in our communal celebrations. My eyes and ears and soul is automatically pleased, shocked, saturated with almost any burst, spray, or boom to get things rolling. I hit the mean early and remain on dazed or flat-lining through what I could never suspect (unless it's sync'd up with "The 1812 Overture") was the penultimate segment, and then all heaven breaks loose: canons, flash-comets, boom bangers, spark sprayers, *waterfalls* of fire—having the last bite be *way* better than the first, *and* being totally unaware of anything being "*almost* last."

In my forties, in therapy, my mentor injected a whole new serum into this stream. Birth order. In this case, I, as a middle born, might be dealing with a proclivity to avoid big completions. Say, with degrees. I notice I have four. Two bachelors and two masters. With *no* Ph.D. I do a couple dozen albums of recorded music and didn't know which was last, much less "next to," till a good while after "all" of them were done. I had no volume number on my first "memoir" book. Maybe I was through. I put a roman numeral "II" on its-up-till then not consciously imagined successor. Opening all doors to at least *numeric* infinity. Should I, or my drive to write thusly, expire before number "III" might appear, my original book will *become* my penultimate offering, in which instance I would rather proclaim it, re-title it, along with Jackson Browne, *My Opening Farewell.*[77] But as things stand now (hey, I'm scratchin' right along with this pen now) it's *possible* it might relinquish that position.

And therein is the glimmer, the lift. "Penultimate" carries with it some hope I'm mistaken. It *could* be *third* to last. Or fifth. Or *last*, in which case a fine fifth would be a good second to last.

All in all though, "second to last" seems worse than "last." With "last" I *know* what I'm dealing with. And that's *all* I'm dealing with. There's a certain freedom in that. There's no more *I* can do. No more efficacy in my struggle. True surrender becomes possible. Peace even. This, whatever it is, begins to feel like the freedom of living a known last day. Maybe just proclaiming everything as "last" would lift the ongoing burden of uncertainty that clouds me, and sirens me away from fuller life. All out engagement. Open to possibles beyond "my" possibles.

The wisdom keepers of all ages have counselled us to look for what is continuous, what is eternal, what does not come and go, appear and disappear. They suggest it is in the "I Am." The "I Amness" I know and am awake to. The I Amness by which God identifies Himself, knows (yes biblically) Herself.

What I can *count on* is not sequential. Transcends time and space.

What I can count on is, "Be still and know that I Am God." Within you.

★   ★   ★

Was that the last of the Breyers?
Help my unbelief.

Last Leaves

There aren't that many
still around
this arid fall
has got them all
quite brown
the ones on branches
much as those
on ground
they shake, the tree ones,
just like palsied
ancient hands
their tentative farewells
assisted ably
by their sister breeze
who taught
them all to dance
so long ago
so why not trust her
with the journey
home

adieu.

John Prine

Hello out there
Hello in there
John
Hello.
And thanks for the family
Sam Stone
Donald and Lydia
Loretta, and the Davy
We lost.
For giving me
Something I can
Hold on to
Flying from my Montgomery's.

I was only "in the room"
With you once
But you were in
My room untold times.
My deep, raw
Human room
Consoled, companioned
Captivated
By your special deliveries
From your well-worn postal bag

To my address
(just when I needed)
Wherever I lived.

I'm especially grateful
For "Father Forgive Us...
You forgive us
We'll forgive you
We'll forgive each other
Till we both turn blue
Then we'll whistle and
Go fishin' in heaven."
From Montgomery
To Mayberry
And back
And forth
Travis pickin'
Me through the
Bitter and the sweet
On the porch
In the street.

Let's rock awhile
Before you retreat
You do the strummin'
I'll do the feet...
I'll see you tonight
When I close my eyes
For a time, for a space, for awhile
Finding home in your face
Your beautiful face
With that cancer-crook'd
Illegal smile.

Joe Wise

Going on 80

Bed Bath and Beyond
The Vicissitudes, Vanities, Victories,
and Other Verities of Elderhood.
Plus Some Other Stuff.

Let's go ahead and start with the "bed, bath, and beyond." Well, with the "bath." Of which, in the last six decades, I have taken, basically—*none*. Ever since it was *my* choice, and the other choice was—*shower*. I know that's probably saved me untold hours (weeks? months?) of time, which I have no doubt spent in dubious activities, with considerably less value than the supreme self-care a bath tenders. Babies and elders. For a lot of us, our bath periods. With help and love. The early ones, welcomed in delight. The later ones calling more for surrender and *allowing* help and love.

There *is* the in between time, when, like Pat Boone, you can open the door, walk right in, sit right down, fill 'er up and whistle "Love Letters in the Sand." Which is just enough longer than two "Happy Birthday to You's" (recommended for thorough hand washing and tooth brushing) just enough longer to get to the rest.

Of course when I say I haven't taken a bath in years, I'm not including the ocean, pool or lake swims. Or hot springs.

Hygiene and rest. Bath and *bed*. Our two mainstays. I find I'm much more in tune with going prone, than any other time in my life. To that end, I have *scheduled in* a *daily* echo of nighttime retiring, a rerun you might say. The nap. Wherein I get to, in the middle of the afternoon, say "good-bye world," and let rest and/or sleep have its way with me again. The world is invariably brighter and friendlier when I rise. At least until I turn on the news—that is broadcast news, a step beyond I-can-skip-this-on-my-homepage news.

A step *beyond*. Ok, after "bed" and "bath," the "beyond." The other rooms? Kitchen. Office. Living room. So far, gratefully, I'm still using *all* of them. The kitchen, mostly to applaud Maleita's latest collage of a meal, wherein lately leftovers often meet newbies, and *I* get to sit and savor the results. The office, where I write sometimes (with pen and paper) when I'm not doing so in a less "distracting" place, like this library. And where I edit always on our home p.c.

The living room contains the most comfortable seat in the house for back-conscious me. And it's there I let audio/visuals round out my experiences in heart and mind and soul by taking me to places I haven't imagined or dared go, and returning me safely to my "most comfortable seat." A room for fuller living. Rendered even fuller when friends come and any and all levels of sharing become possible.

I get to throw in a garage and a laundry room here. Came with my current home. A laundry room, which holds the machines and racks I need, to be the household's laundry person. That precious activity that has the mercy and satisfaction of a clear beginning, middle and end, folded into the gift of tending to the many fabrics that house my spouse's body. And a garage for housing my car, which gratefully I can still drive, and thereby experience the mobility and freedom of life outside my "home" rooms. *That* beyond, which has recently included teaching my *favorite* (and only) grandchild/ daughter, Alicia, 15 (and 50) mid-teener and crone, in from Denver, and ready to roll, teaching Alicia to drive.

My goal was to get her comfortable going on 80 (mph). My exact goal with my age (yoe).[78] Ten, she told me was her top speed in the limited forays she'd had in Littleton. Eleven days of intensives and a couple of trials-by-fire (one literally, encountering a huge brush fire that shut down I-17 both ways overnight) eleven days, two trials, and it was mission accomplished. Highlighted by a (number two) night drive in a light drizzle on an interstate with an eighteen mile downgrade, in a townless dark-skies zone, newly surfaced black, and as yet, without lines. Some 18 wheelers gave up completely and shoulder-stopped, while "Captain Alicia" announced, as she passed them, "That's right, truckers, go ahead and pull over, while the young prodigy whizzes on by." If I wasn't so petrified, I would have laughed.

By extreme contrast, the day after Alicia arrived, I took an elderly (*my* age) woman to a doctor's appointment on the same road. She had not been on an interstate since she was t-boned by a distracted driver and sustained life changing injuries. As I entered the long downgrade in broad daylight and came up behind my first big truck and was about to swing out and pass him (at near 80 in a 75 zone) she said she was scared and could I slow down. I could. I did. Sixty was her highest "comfort" speed. We were then locked and "rocked in the cradle" (as they call it) with the truckers.

An emerging woman speeding up. An elder woman slowing down. I seemed to be as much a student as anybody in these adventures. With Alicia though, way beyond lessons, I was invited into, given something beyond measure. In a culture of few markers or rituals for a young one "coming of age," where outright mentoring and fostering are prized, this stands as one. And living 800 miles away, she came, and for eleven days we engaged in that. She reminded me of all this in an email, a note she sent me…right after she drove her mother home ("on the way least scary for Mom") from Denver International Airport…at midnight. A great "*beyond*."

Meanwhile back at the ranch, back to the room to room, and looking at our *exit* from all these rooms (*that* "beyond") looking at our exit, as we "of a certain age" are wont to do, I have two scenarios that come to me. The first described by an old friend, Jim Flynn, who tended to his father in his final days. He saw his Dad's passage as a slow surrender of room, after room, after room till only the bedroom remained, where he passed. The second, Paul Mathews, Maleita's Dad, who after several heart events, said he wanted to die in his tomato patch. The big sky room. He did. A quick event. The day before Easter.

That sounds pretty good to me. The being active part especially. And the big sky room. Doing something I love. Right now, that would most likely translate as a holiday for all the students at Mingus High, because I died on their track before classes, where, and when, I run. This (with anonymous runner-dude me) has the bonus of an immediate *mass* celebration. *No school today!*

The next closest alternative for me would be writing. At *this* library at Yavapai College, Clarkdale or my "home" one in Cottonwood. My only concern here would be, *what was I writing?* I could only hope it would be an exploration of some deep philosophical psycho/social issue, illuminated by all 80 of my years on the planet. But, if it's my grocery list, I'd like for my last word to be: *Breyers.*

You'd think all my concerns around (and I love this term) "impression management" would have dried up (like my skin) and blown away (like half my hair) by now. I feel like I'm becoming the living proof you can never be too old for vanities. I have *some* victories in that department. The hair I have left is still its natural color. My beard, not so much. It's just too white for my inner youth.

Well, they're closing up the library now. I have to leave *this* room. I've been given the 10 minute warning, considerably more civil than the 2 minute warning the NFL maintains. And just in case *this* is the last thing I will ever write,

> *I want to wish all you pre-octogenarians godspeed and safe travel toward the summit, whatever you conceive that to be, and may you have great and true companions all along Life's way.*

> Sincerely,
> Breyers

P.S. As I write this, word has just come out that "Bed Bath and Beyond" is going to be no more. It's closing. It's heading for the beyond. Even sooner than me.[79]

80

Ain't he great, he
Made it to 80.

With a little help
From the Life Force
Who did all the magic.

For my part:

Some discipline
Some genes
Some kale
Some beans.

More beans
Some toots
Some nuts
Some fruits.

Some teeth
Some hair
Some *life*
Down *there.*

Some nature
Some nurture
Some lifting
Some rupture.

My *skin*'s acting funny
Gone crinkled and crepey
My butt's goin' South
Re-inventing its...shapey??

Drivin' the *roads*
With daring and ease
Ever' time I remember
Where I left the keys.

Never need a *map*
Who *knows* how to fold it?
Still off my rocker
Ever since I sold it.

Gave up my dreams
For Porsches and Cadillacs
Crowned 2 *molars* instead,
Had 'em fish out my cataracts.

Went to my derm doc
He froze off some skin
My Cologuard came
I'm mailin' *it* in.

My spiritual growth?
I'm doin' just fine.
Ever' *day* I wake *up*
And *again* lose my mind.

Joe Wise

Still reading
Still writing
Still napping
Exciting.

My mind is still nimble
It jumps all around
Making up rhymes
Do you have any sasparilli?
I know it sounds silly
And funny…
And…
OMG
I forgot about *fun*.
Where *are* my keys?
Screw 81.

That Bird

I had my foot
Atop a good sized
Rock to stretch
The long and strong
Assemblage that
Rides behind the
Two bones of my
One leg
The "Left" by name
Co-equal prime
Mover of my
Frame over earth.
With Mr. "Right."

The visiting middle school
Track coach,
With his team,
Let me use lane 6, this
Brisk morning at
Mingus High.

I was having
A "Rocky Mingus High"
Cool down stretch
Just now re-joined

In a neighboring tree
By my early
Morning mate
Mr. Raven
Solo me on earth
Solo he in sky
Before the young'uns came.

And then...
A flash of movement
Out of foliage
Left to right...
Never before, in 16 years here...
My mind said,
Oh, there's a...
I fished and fished
And fished hard
In the reservoir of re-call.
Nothing.
Relax.
Then—"Hummingbird."
Relief.
Then...If I could
Hear better, maybe
I could've "heard"
Her "hum?"
Losing cells I am.
Here and there
Hear and there.
Putting me in a cell?

Maybe, it's my invitation
To stop running so much
And open more
To the wonder and beauty

Of all beingness
Before the name.
Connecting less with brain
And more with heart.

I am remembering
A good friend, Ben,
Who in his days of
Mental recession
Once took my hand
And one of my wife's
Looked us deeply
And long in the eyes
And said, "I know I
Know you. And we have
Been close." I choose
To believe his eyes
Said, "Same Love."

I am remembering
A good poet teacher
Unmet friend
Named Cat
And now Josuf,
Taking my ear and heart
And saying,
      "If I ever lose my eyes...
           I won't have to cry
    If I ever lose my legs...
           I won't have to walk
    My mouth...
           I won't have to talk"
These are not who I am.

Then taught me the prayer
That goes with
This losing.
      "Did (Will) it take long to
      Find me?"
      I asked the faithful Light.
      Did (Will) it take long to
      Find me...
      And are you gonna'
      Stay the night."[80]

I now add,
And stay the day,
As well.
And, help me know
All ways
What does *not*
Come or go.

The World is Big

The world is big
The sky is vast
The sands innumerable
Rock sculptures infinite
Oceans unfathomable.
My cup is small,

But my formless heart
Has room for it all—
And then some.

Including this burst I know
As "flower."

An Adventure Not Taken

This is from my writers group. The prompt: An Adventure You Didn't Take. Twenty minutes with pen.

I have not gone to the Redwoods. To be with the Sequoias.

I know I can *be* with them "from here." I can be with anything from here. It's not the same as being form to form. In my 81st year I'm becoming more and more conscious of big things, and old things—the bigger and older the better. Zenithing out, I suppose, with the Universe or Multiverse itself. I recall Carl Sagan's[81] response to someone who asked him how to make an apple pie. "You begin by making a universe."

I'm still, and expect to be still, till I die—still big on form to form presence. My ocean thirst got slaked, surprisingly and wonderfully, by a friend's gift, a week at his condo on the Jersey shore, a couple of years ago. The Mingus Mountains are big and old enough for me. Sedona's red rocks are ancient and beautiful enough for me.

I still want to *stand* with, by, *sit* with, by, a giant tree of some antiquity. Sit on roots that have centuries of transferring life, health, nourishment and grounding, all around stability to its above-earth self. I will introduce my soul to such a form with all its hidden fountains. I will stand next to what it feeds. Skin to bark. Beyond the hug's reach, yet I will spread my tiny wings as wide as they have ever gone, and go as silent as the being that, no matter the picture, embraces *me*.

Finish Strong

"Finish Strong."

I was just *starting*. Cold a.m. Layered transporter, my body. Gloved and head-banded. My glance catches the command (exhortation?) now familiar to my morning eyes, "Finish Strong," writ large, painted actually, on the clubhouse here at Bright Field, home of the Mingus Marauders, home of my thousands of miles (at least 11k of them) with my one-member frequent runners club. Not many venture out here this early. My main track buddy, Reuben, teaches and drives a school bus here. So until the weekend or holidays or summer, I only get to wave to him, going out to gather his charges, and coming back to deposit them for another day of whatever teens do in school these days. Part of my ritual here is to wave to *all* the drivers coming and going. I only "know" two of the yellow-shelled taxiers, but every once in a while, at the supermarket or Walmart (Cottonwood's town square) or on a sidewalk, someone will stop me and say "hey, you're the runner who waves to me," and proceed to tell me what it means to them. I am always moved. Their gift to *me* is getting to connect with another soul in my solitary endeavor. Their gift to *us*, taking care of our kids, teens, young adults.

This morning, in January, the sun is low on the horizon and is not "up" (above the rim) yet. It *will* be during my second mile (of five). There is enough muted field light to see the track, its lanes, and the "Finish Strong." With the sun's light will come my most faithful track buddies, the Ravens. The elegant big ones, and the industrious little ones. They don't try to interpret the "Finish Strong."

I do. I'm a "word guy" (a verb-o-phile). My favorite pointers. To Truth, and how I might "arrive" at it. And as help, on the "way."

O.K. "Finish Strong." My first few laps are getting my breath and rhythm, and usually having my zaniest thoughts or dialogues drop by at will.

Finish strong.

What's that? Spinach thong? Well, that was Adam's swimming suit or BVD's.

I don't give a fig what it was.

"Finish Strong." Colonel Sanders did—starting at 65, sold a gazillion buckets of chicken, right before he kicked it. Madame Currie did—able to "table" new elements right up to the end. James Patterson is at a *gallop* now, even though with a bevy of relay partners, Bill Clinton the latest.

And *Tony Bennett was just at the Grammies.*

What's that? A phony tenant at my Grammy's? Can't be. No, she's dead, not rentin' any more.

"Finish Strong." I guess the idea here is to run *through* the tape. Not *to* it. Don't celebrate till the end zone. Lest you get "tortoised" by a hair.

You mean a bunny?

No, I mean a follicle, or what's attached to it.

How about, just plain "Finish"?

What's that? Just playin' quiddich?

Hogwarts! Never heard of it.

★ ★ ★

The next few laps are usually open for deeper reflection, or if I'm lucky and aware, just beingness. Both of these presuming some major (or mind-made major) issue or event is not taking over the whole run.

"Finish." What is so satisfying about "finishing?" H'mm...I get to *call it.* The siren song of *control* calls me, and in the face of the daily great unknown, *I* call the *finish*. I say and set what is "successful." I *call it*, the goal.

"Finish strong." Hey, I'm still buying green bananas. To finish *anything* is "good."

There *is* something about running measurable distances or climbing measurable heights some of us must find comforting. Some validation of our courage or persistence or fidelity. Maybe all three. Some kinesthetic validation of our excellence. As a physical entity, and perhaps transferable to our *persona* as well. One thing about running that is not speculative for me: I like the endorphins. It just *feels* good. Like my Honda, with an oil and lube and tire rotation.

We who walk (or run) in the Double Realm, the one of form and the one of formlessness, seeking to calm ourselves, and fortify ourselves in the face of uncertain time and space and even purpose, relish the *repetitive*. The comfort of it, the predictive nature of it, the mind-freezing gift of it. The next footfall, the next oar pull, pedal, stitch, the next prayer bead. Letting go of everything, or most everything in the form world, freeing ourselves to access the boundless, the non-physical, the transcendent, all in this moment of physical action. Finding stillness on the move.

Once I found five miles was my most satisfying distance, and once I got old enough to more easily injure myself running roads (joints over time) or (my favorite) trails (body parts quickly), I found, and was *blessed* to find, *tracks*. Even one in my small hometown. Mingus Union High has been my "home," along with a level loop at Windmill Park down the road, for the last two decades of my running. The track *was* a dirt composite (to be generous) till just a few years ago, when all heaven broke loose and delivered a modern, alchemized, cushioned, leg-friendly 8 lane miracle. My tax dollars contributed to the birth and delivery. Sooo…it's open, during all non-school hours (even midnight) to *me*. Pre-Columbine, I ran anytime. During practices, drills, P.E., everything but games. Now, with safety decisions, it's A.M. Early A.M. Today, *cold* A.M.

To give myself the freedom to access my spirit and its realm, as well as that of the body, I needed to come up with some way to "get my 5 in" without squandering a great deal of mind space or fumbling with click counters for laps. As a poet, rhymes came to me. As a free-willed being, changing directions entered the mix, four laps one way, then four the other, along with lane switching, and finally an honoring of an "outer lanes only" request by the "trackmaster" to keep all the inner ones least worn for track meets. With the lane number, direction, and rhymes at each lap's beginning, there's *just enough* mind play for me and a broad opening for my soul.

Number one, runner's fun. Number three, lucky me. Number six, runner's kicks. I don't finish, strong or otherwise, till 18. The firemen, who train here, have "mapped out" a 5 mile journey in lane 1, and one in lane 8. 20 laps in lane one, the inside lane, and 17 and1/2 in the outside lane, lane 8. My lane-changing sequence comes to 18.

My middle laps have a strong focus on affirming body and soul meditative states. *Number eight, feeling great. Nine...feeling fine.*

Number 16 is a big shift for me. I couldn't think of a good rhyme for it, so I settled on: *Sixteen. Sweet.* An age at which many of us begin to mellow a little bit, and come to believe there is something more than *turbulence* in our adolescence, in our teens, in our *life*, while also becoming more attuned to *others*, who we more and more recognize are in the same boat, on the same sea, on the same trip. The "big shift" for me on this lap is moving my attention from me to my fellow travelers. It takes the form of the Buddhist practice of *tonglen*.

I call to mind (soul) someone I know, and say (pray) *May he be free from suffering and the roots of suffering.* This may be the totality of my prayer for someone I am having trouble forgiving. I can usually say this much with integrity about anyone who comes to mind. The rest is, *May she be happy. May she be well.* My final three laps usually find me connecting this way with this practice in "my circle." Near and far. I let them appear. Sometimes a world leader sneaks in. Sometimes a checker or cashier I don't know by name. *All* the bus drivers. And all of this ends with, *May I be free from suffering and the roots of suffering. May I be happy and well.* Lest I, in some fashion, as pray-er forget *I* am part of the race, the human race, and the larger family of sentient beings.

"Finish Strong." This one's been on the wall for *two* years now. I stopped the coach one morning and asked him why this one stayed up more than one season. He said the *painters* never got to it. The actual rallying cry and motivator for this year's squad: "On Us."

"Oh," I say to myself, "this second year has been for *me*." Me in my finishing years. My long ago therapist, and finest mentor, told me in our final (phone) conversation, on his finishing earth-lap (four years ago now) "It all went by so fast."

It's starting to pick up "speed" for *me*. I am reminded of one of his teachings. "You're never gonna get it *all* done." It was/is a handmaiden to his, "You will know much peace when you accept that in life you will get *some* of the all." I now add, "And trust the *selection* to Source." In this second month of my 80th year on the planet, I know my 18 laps will not be "going by" fast. It never was about that for me. Speed. I keep or have no records. Not even personal bests.

I don't want to finish weak, I don't want to finish strong. I want to finish with no judgement on which is better, even on which is which. I want to finish free from suffering and the roots of suffering. Happy and well. I want *you* to, too.

As for the realism of getting "*all the way*" there on this trip, surely there's *something* between a "whimper" and a "bang."

★　★　★

The sound track for this piece, for me, would certainly be Neil Diamond's:

Jesus Christ, Fanny Brice
Wolfgang Mozart, Humphrey Bogart...
Ho Chi Min, Gunga Din
Henry Luce and John Wilkes Booth...
Ramar Krishna, Mama Whistler...
E.A. Poe, Henri Rousseau...
Alan Freed and Buster Keaton too

And each one there
Has one thing shared
They have sweated beneath the same sun
Looked up in wonder at the same moon
And wept when it was all done
For bein' done too soon
For bein' done too soon
For bein' done...[82]

Sweater Me

Sweater me, O God,
In the autumn
Of my life.
Pull, at last,
Your wool
Over my eyes.

I will always lean
          My heart
As close to your soul
          As I can.
                    Hafiz

Also by Joe Wise

Albums:

Gonna Sing My Lord, 1966
Hand in Hand, 1968
A New Day, 1970
Sweet Water, 1970
Watch With Me, 1972
Welcome In, 1973
Take It For Gift, 1975
Take All the Lost Home, 1977
He Has Come, Songs for Christmas, 1977
Songs for the Journey, 1978
Lights of the City (with **Ed Gutfreund and John Pell**), 1979
And the Light Shines, 1982
Most Requested, Music for the Spirit, 1994
Most Requested, Music for the Spirit, Volume II, 2003

Children's Albums:

Close Your Eyes, 1974
Show Me Your Smile, 1976
Pockets, 1978
Doodle Bee Do, 1981

Don't Say Cheese, 1987
The Best of Joe Wise...Music for Kids, 1987
The Best of Joe Wise...Music for Kids Volume 2, 2003

Books:

The Body at Liturgy (no longer in print) 1972
Songprints, (a photo/poem essay), 1973
Through a Glass Lightly, (poems and essays), 1987★
The Truth in Twenty, 2013★
The Truth in Plenty, 2017★
Finding My Way, 2021★

Film Score:

A Time to Die, 1970

★　　★　　★

Most albums (collections or single songs as downloads) and music books, available at <u>www.giamusic.com</u>, iTunes, and Amazon. The 2 *Most Requested* albums and the 2 *Best of Music for Kids* albums, as well as the *Pockets* album, are also available as CDs. *Through a Glass Lightly* and all sheet music at giamusic.com.

About the Author

Joe's music has been known and sung around the world since the mid 60's. His four degrees are in Philosophy, Theology, Education, and Counseling and Guidance. For the first 22 years of his work life he wrote music, recorded it and performed it; gave lectures, conducted workshops, and facilitated retreats—throughout the U.S. and Canada, as well as in Europe, Australia, and New Zealand.

Wise has been a resident of Arizona since 1995. Before that he lived 55 years in Louisville, Kentucky where between travels he offered a variety of workshops on writing and video story- telling, including as facilitator with other artists at the Louisville Visual Artist Association and Bellarmine College.

His painting career has included studies with many accomplished artists including Ed Hermann and Joe Fettingis. His primary mentor was Dick Phillips. Joe is a member of the Sedona Visual Artists Coalition and a charter and juried member of the Northern Arizona Watercolor Society. His paintings have received numerous awards and hang in corporate headquarters and private collections.

He has written, produced, and recorded 22 albums of music, published 6 books and scored a film. He has worked for over a dozen years teaching writing as a therapeutic tool in treatment centers for addictions, and conducts retreats using the journal as a gateway for spiritual awareness and clarity. Joe lives with his wife Maleita in the Sedona area of Northern Arizona. He travels out presenting readings of his works, some song, and reflections on the grand mix of life.

Joe can be contacted at: <u>wise1@q.com</u>
or through: www.joeandmaleitawise.com

Endnotes

1   Enjoy his work at www.larrylindahl.com.

2   Lakota prayer.

3   See his many works at www.garyevery.com.

4   Extended to 9:29 during the Derek Chauvin trial in the death of George Floyd.

5   From her presidential inaugural presentation, January, 2021 and in her new book, *The Hill We Climb,* release date, March 30ᵗʰ, 2021. From Penguin Random House.

6   From Robert Browning's "Pippa's Song."

7   See William Blake's poem, "Eternity."

8   The 1967 Jimmy Webb song recorded by the 5ᵗʰ Dimension. Placed #43 on BMI's "Top 100 songs of the century." Later appearing on *his* 1977 album, *JT.*

9   It includes this verse:

> Now the thing about time
> Is that time isn't real.
> It's all on your point of view.
> How does it feel for you?
> Einstein said that he could
> Never understand it all; planets
> Spinning through space
> The smile upon your face.
> Welcome to the human race.

10 As it turned out, this was re-scheduled for the first Saturday in September, instead of the 1ˢᵗ Saturday of May. The first change in scheduling in 146 years.

11 Sung by Dean Martin, the song, "That's Amoré," first appeared in the soundtrack of the movie, *The Caddy,* released in 1953. The first verse of which is, "When the moon hits your eye like a big pizza pie, that's amoré."

12 "Sally go round the roses." A 1963 hit by the Jaynettes, a Bronx-based one-hit wonder girl group, on the Tuff label.

13 We both shared a love of Gregorian chant. The beauty, simplicity, and mystic nature of it. I was a cantor in my seminary's choir. We also shared an appreciation of classic polyphonic choir offerings. His request shocked me, even though I knew from experience he was fond of folk music. I didn't know of anybody else, in the very early 60s, using guitar and folk-like music in church ceremonies.

14 He sang, unbelievably, the Elvis version!

15 I know it was with delight that he gave his treasured Cassel's German-English Dictionary to one of my two oldest (since 1945) dear friends as he left for studies at Notre Dame. Bob still speaks warmly of the gift.

16 Though at a level or two below the "11 secret herbs and spices" in KFC, headquartered in our city.

17 We had, Johnny, Maggie and I, held something more than a tentative vision of opening a married couples retreat center. And conducting the programs.

18 One piece of which, was one day "hearing" him say, of the window, "Are you kidding me? C'mon now, get a grip here. Lighten up!"

19 After ten and a half years in the whole program. Starting in high school. With glowing reviews sent to Monsignor as my pastor by my faculties throughout the years.

20 Romans 8:28. *He* had underlined "All."

21 I think it is important to note here, in this the era of uncovering clergy sexual abuse, that I never experienced even a hint of that with Monsignor. Or, gratefully, from any priest, in my journey to maturity.

22 And could maybe even venture a tentative handshake with Professor Karl.

23 Or some kind of senior fostering.

24 Penguin Books, 2011.

25 Dog on a ledge? Stop, Joe

26 Since my move to Arizona, I talk to Eric and Margie before and after the game. Now just Margie, since Eric's passing in March of 2018.

27 And of course it goes without mention you take any drop-down oxygen mask first, before attending to any other family member or guest in the room with (overt or covert) traitorous allegiances. They knew it was a *Wild*-cat before they jumped ship.

28 Written by David Barrett about the NCAA division I Men's Basketball Tourney. First aired by CBS with a recording by Teddy Pendergrass, but known by most as Luther Vandross's version, played after the championship game.

29 It sported a distinctive five-pointed-star logo displayed on the high top's ankle patch, and incorporated Chuck Taylor's signature in the design. I did

discover Chuck's real identity as a player and later a basketball shoe salesman/ product marketer from Brown County Indiana, after writing this piece.

30 Joe Dean, known as "Mr. String Music" was the voice of S.E.C. basketball for most of the 1970s-80s. He introduced this phrase into the broadcaster's lexicon to describe a shooter's swishing success.

31 Shortstop for the Brooklyn and L.A. Dodgers from 1940-58. Ten time all-star. Inducted into Hall of Fame in 1984. Also known for his support of his teammate, Jackie Robinson, the first African American player in the major leagues' modern era, especially in Jackie's difficult first years.

32 It's possible he's John Arthur Fitzpatrick. Anybody know? Write me at wise1@q.com.

33 The theme song for The Harlem Globetrotters.

34 Lonzo Ball's Z02 basketball shoes. Sold by his family's Big Baller Brand. "Father Ball(er)" tweeted: "If you can't afford the Z02s, you're not a BIG BALLER." Mercy.

35 Length of shot clock when this was penned.

36 The reservation.

37 Even as I saw his people's Way as wonderfully inclusive, earth centered, arising from nature, sacramental, ancient and "complete." My go to prayer chant is Native American: "Oh Great Spirit, earth sun sky and sea, you are inside, and all around me."

38 In the 80's and long before widespread cell phone use.

39 Dick passed in July of 2011. He attended this opening and I got to "embarrass" him in my presentation of this piece. He never wanted you to paint like anybody but yourself. He just kept "supplying" the tools. And encouragement. And mirth. His work was recently included in the Arts in Embassies Program sponsored by the United States Department of State. Can't think of a better rep. He is listed in the *Who's Who in American Art*. And in my heart.

40 Was this the "Boateater?" We were definitely not a mixed "meal." I never saw or felt any of my "foursome." Or the boat. Or rocks or rock walls. A solitary experience in every way.
I had no awareness of water temperature.

41 Henry John Deutschendorf, Jr. Known professionally as John Denver.

42 Lyrics by Eleanor Farjeon, (1881-1965). Music by Cat Stevens (Yusuf Islam).

43 Song title and lyric from the rock ballad written and performed by Aerosmith for the movie *Armageddon*.

44 "Bread and Wine," from my album *And the Light Shines*. Also on the *Most Requested, Music for the Spirit* CD.

45 From the book and title of the same name, *Vaster than Sky, Greater than Space*, by the Jamaican spiritual teacher based in Portugal, Anthony Paul Moo-Young, now known as Mooji.

46 These last being mostly the words we associate with "name-calling."

47 And needs to be in session at a moment's notice, reflexively, for our safety especially.

48 See davidrothmusic.com.

49 Matthew 20:1-16.

50 Hamlet Act 2, scene 2, 239-251.

51 Of course there's "baaad" and "bad-ass," which actually mean "good." Go figure.

52 Buddhism has helpful teachings about "right" speech. The works of Pema Chödrön are my "go to" favorites.

53 This trip is in the late 1980s. Not long after this writing I became a cellphone owner, with the hope that I would remain the "owner" in the "relationship."

54 Reminding me of a quote I could stick on a mental postcard and send to myself often: "Having a wonderful time. Wish I was here."

55 It also helps me and challenges me, to throw in this suggestion from Brother David Steindl-Rast, "Consider nothing in your day as an interruption."

56 Pre-cellphone days.

57 They're out of the "attic" now. Though not hanging, I know where they are. I'm better at appreciating what I do.

58 From the Traveler Insurance Company's ads circa 1980-90s, featuring the red umbrella and "You're better off under the umbrella."

59 Now known as a gambling destination. Pre casinos it was home to the Blackhawk Mountain School of Art, and co-run by Michelle's first art teacher/mentor/inspirer, Bob Lockhart. See https://www.pyrogallery.com/bob-lockhart-artist.

60 "She Came from Fort Worth," written by Pat Alger and Fred Koller. Released as a single in April 1990, from the album *Willow in the Wind*.

61 "Seasons in the Sun" is an English-language adaptation of the 1961 song "Le Moribond," by Jacqes Brel, sung by Terry Jacks.

62 From the song "Michelle," written by Paul McCartney with a "middle eight" help from John Lennon, released on the Album *Rubber Soul*, 1965.

63 See the last verse of "80" a little further into this collection.

64 Written by Michael Martin Murphy.

65 With tutelage from a favorite cousin, Mark Brian.

66 Recording on *The Best of Joe Wise Music for Kids*, vol.1. Appearing originally on the album *Pockets*.

67 Hawaiian for "John."

68 1892-1964, American spiritual author, teacher and modern day mystic, who studied the scriptures in their original texts.

69 Of course there is no locus and every locus to this Presence. I resonate fully with the native American chant:
"O Great Spirit, Earth sun sky and sea. You are inside, and all around me."

70 Sometimes "leela." In the Advaitic Hindu tradition leela signifies play and freedom as distinguished from necessity.

71 These are temporal opposites. Presence, Life has no opposite, no clock.

72 And don't even get me started on the 4258s, the mega millions super jackpot, Rainiers, that are even *more* rare, and a car payment to purchase.

73 The deuteragonist of the *Karate Kid* film series, played by Pat Morita.

74 From *Songprints*, a photo poem essay, co-authored by Joe Wise and David Duffin, with sound track by John Pell.

75 From his *Rhymes and Reasons* album, 1969.

76 Sri Nisargadatta Maharaj.

77 Long one of my favorite songs. His *first* released song. In 1972. The YouTube presentation with Bonnie Raitt is my favorite performance.

78 Yoe. Years on earth.

79 It turns out they will just be closing a few hundred stores. The report was precipitous, as I hope mine will be for some time, so that for a while I can declare, with one of my all-time favorite writers, Samuel Clemens, "Rumors of my demise have been greatly exaggerated."
    Which somehow always reminds me of *this* from Groucho Marx, "I've had a perfectly wonderful evening, but this wasn't it."

80 "Moonshadow" by Jusuf Islam/Cat Stevens (born Steven Demetre Georgiou), from the album *Teaser and the Firecat*, 1971.

81 20th century American astronomer, planetary scientist, cosmologist.

82 "Done Too Soon." From *Tap Root Manuscript* 1970. In the early 70's I was asked to teach a graduate course at the Illif School of Theology in Denver. This collection was my syllabus.